THE BUSINESS WRITING COACH

Patrick Forsyth

The Teach Yourself series has been trusted around the world for over 60 years. It has helped millions of people improve their skills and achieve their goals. This new 'Coach' series of business books is created especially for people who want to focus proactively on a specific workplace skill and to get a clear result at the end of it. Whereas many business [illegible] the Coach will help you walk the walk.

Teach Yourself®

THE BUSINESS WRITING COACH

Patrick Forsyth

First published in Great Britain in 2015 by Hodder & Stoughton. An Hachette UK company.

First published in US in 2015 by The McGraw-Hill Companies, Inc.

British Library Cataloguing in Publication Data: a catalogue record for this title is available from the British Library.

Library of Congress Catalog Card Number: on file

Paperback ISBN 978 1 47360 884 9

1

Typeset by Cenveo Publisher Services.

Printed and bound in Great Britain by CPI Group (UK) Ltd., Croydon CRO 4YY.

John Murray Learning policy is to use papers that are natural, renewable and recyclable products and made from wood grown in sustainable forests. The logging and manufacturing processes are expected to conform to the environmental regulations of the country of origin.

Hodder & Stoughton Ltd

338 Euston Road

London NW1 3BH

www.hodder.co.uk

CONTENTS

'One should aim not at being possible to understand, but at being impossible to misunderstand.'

Quintilian, Roman rhetorician

MEET THE COACH

Patrick Forsyth is a consultant, trainer and writer and runs Touchstone Training & Consultancy based in the UK. His background is in marketing and he works mainly to improve communication skills: sales, negotiation, making effective presentations and more. In training (he has conducted a range of training, varying from individual tuition to in-company and public courses and seminars in many industries and in various overseas locations as well as the UK) he has regularly addressed the subject of business writing in all its forms.

To draw attention to poor writing standards he spent a couple of years collecting examples of a variety of errors – ranging from the warning on a packet of prescription sleeping tablets ('may cause drowsiness') to amusingly confusing road signs ('It is dangerous to cross this bridge when this notice is underwater'). The resulting book, *Empty When Half Full* (Rethink Press), has been described as 'hilarious', though it presents sobering lessons too.

He has written widely on business topics and has many successful business books including three other books in the Teach Yourself series: *Outstanding Confidence In A Week*, *Successful Direct Marketing In A Week* and *Successful Pitching For Business In A Week*. Thus, on the topic here at least, he aims to practise what he preaches: one reviewer says of his work – 'Patrick has a lucid and elegant style of writing which allows him to present information in a way that is organized, focused and easy to apply.' (*Professional Marketing* magazine).

He can be contacted at www.patrickforsyth.com

HOW TO USE THIS BOOK

Outcomes from this chapter: this box, which you will find at the beginning of each chapter, explains what you will get from the chapter.

Online resource: these boxes will contain complementary online resources for you to download free of charge and make use of.

COACHING SESSION

Coaching session: this book will be filled with practical 'sessions' consisting of self-assessment quizzes, diagnostic tools, tables to fill in, free-form space to write in, checklists and more to help you improve.

Coach's tip: these are personal tips from the author to motivate you to success.

Next steps: at the end of each chapter you will find a summary of what you have learned and what you have done in the chapter, and what comes next.

Takeaways: there will also be a section consisting of three or four questions at the end of the chapter. You will need to write in the answer and reflect more deeply on what you have done in the chapter and what you remember.

1 INTRODUCTION

This chapter sets the scene: it will help you appreciate that the task of business writing can be difficult, yet see that it is possible to put over a clear message if you go about it the right way. It also sets out how this book will take you through the topic and help you to relate its content and lessons to your own work.

Putting a clear message in writing can sometimes be difficult; it is the mission of this book to make it easier for you. As we start, consider this, a sign on the inside of hotel room doors: 'In the interest of security please ensure that your door is fully closed firmly before entering or leaving your room.' It's a good trick if you can do it, but the message is anything but clear.

THE COMMUNICATION CHALLENGE

The example above makes a point: someone not only wrote this, they had it printed and posted on more than 200 doors and apparently still didn't notice that it was nonsense.

In the workplace, and elsewhere too, successful communication can often be difficult; and poor communication can cause problems. This may involve a momentary hiatus as two people try to sort out exactly what was meant. Or it may cause a major misunderstanding that leads to a project of some sort being stopped in its tracks or a reputation to crumble.

Why is this? There are many reasons, but one is certainly an assumption that what is being done is surely not difficult; for the most part we muddle through and hope to get there somehow in the end. If we don't, and if breakdowns in communication continue to occur, then some rethinking may prove useful.

Furthermore, some kinds of communication are inherently more difficult than others. The intentions of communication may vary. It may need to inform, explain, motivate, challenge, prompt a debate or more; and such intentions are not mutually exclusive: one communication may need to do several of these things at once. It may well prove difficult just to succeed in even the simplest of these.

Perhaps a message is simply superfluous, like the motorway sign saying: 'This sign is not in use.' Sometimes the message may be muddled, but the true meaning can be inferred, as with the sign at the zoo that said: 'Bring one child and another goes free' (what? released into the wild?). Or the health and safety newsletter's item about bouncy castles under the heading: 'Inflatable children's play equipment.'

It might also be affected by moving from one language to another as was presumably the case with the notice in the bathroom of a hotel in Portugal which said: 'Please ensure that mat is affixed firmly to bottom before entering shower.'

On other occasions messages may end up meaningless...

'To talk about information is to talk about objectives. A lot of thought is now being applied throughout the NHS to mission statements and objectives, from which we should obtain a clearer view of our information needs. However, objectives will never stand still, and therefore an information strategy will of necessity be a continuously developing concept. The process of clarification will be incremental, and the concept of a definitive strategy will remain illusory.'

Yes, well, passing over the idea of objectives never standing still, this simply gets lost amid its own pretensions. It is from a Regional Health Authority report quoted in the press.

Sometimes, too, it is the pretension that seems to produce the over-engineering. For example this description – 'a new and improved pest control system that utilizes a percussive device with a planar surface and orthogonal contoured extension to instantly kill insects stone dead'. What?

It means hitting the insect with a hammer when it is on a flat surface! So, any communicating clearly needs some care. Even when care is being taken additional complications may contrive to compound the problems.

There is a further problem, and that is that most people are better at communicating face to face than in other ways. Other methods do have their disadvantages.

The telephone is good, immediate, maybe quick and easy, but try describing to someone over the telephone how to, say, tie a shoelace. Think about it for a second. You know how to do it, you could show someone else – but, on the telephone, using only your voice, it is somehow more of a challenge.

CURIOUSLY DIFFICULT

People tend to be rendered less articulate when they have to put something in writing. Your manager wants a note about it, the board needs a report or proposal, my editor wants a book (and there are still some 50,000 words to go!).

Business writing almost seems to hinder good communication. People who can talk about something, and usually get their message over successfully, find themselves descending into a muddle and writing something that is over-formal, over-long and – at worst – forgetting somewhere along the way exactly what their initial objectives were. Technical matters and technology make things worse.

This: 'We provide the leading business-to-business solution for clinical data capture and management for the pharmaceutical and biotech industry', probably means, 'We streamline processes to speed important new drug therapies to market.'

'If the style is archaic, the language is labyrinthine; if it is replete with sesquipedalians, places its full points over long distances apart and allows an element of galimatias to act to confuse and obscure the sense – and another thing, it is without structure...' Sorry, try again.

'If you write something full of long words, long sentences, and that has no recognizable structure to guide you through, it is likely to fail.' Incidentally, sesquipedalian is a long word (takes one to know one I suppose) and galimatias is 'gibberish/gobbledygook'. I know it says on the book's cover that there would be no – inappropriate – long words used in this book and here are two before we even reach Chapter 2; but they are only there to illustrate what to avoid. Just to get all this out of the way, 'hippopotomonstrosesquipedaliophobia' is a fear of long words; perhaps an early lesson for all business writers.

Even one wrong decision can render a written document ineffective. For example, consider this case: in a new job and charged with making radical changes, Mary found every plan she put forward to her boss was rejected. An examination of the tone of her proposals showed why. She was writing something like the following – 'This system is not working well and could be corrected by...' albeit coupled with a perfectly sensible suggestion.

But who had originated the system she planned to change? Her boss. In effect she was saying: 'Your system's no good, I can suggest something better.' A change of tone to one that positioned the change carefully in time terms – 'This system has worked well in the past; in future we must find a way of also accommodating... so building in the following changes will...' reversed the reaction.

It was only the implied criticism of past action that produced the negative reaction. A minor change to the way such a proposal was written was enough to change the way it was received. Such seemingly minor matters are often instrumental in dictating outcomes

Putting something into written form can be a chore, made doubly agonizing over the choice of best form of words. Hence this book: the intention here is clear. It is to assist the process of communicating successfully when it must be done in writing.

This may mean a letter, an email, or it may mean a report, a proposal or a document. It might also mean copy for a brochure or a newsletter. A message may be sent internally: to a group of staff or an individual member of a manager's team – or upwards, perhaps to your manager. It may be sent externally: to a supplier or a customer. The circumstances can vary. But the intention is always the same. It is to put across a message to someone else that will be understood, that will achieve its purpose and that will perhaps impress in the process.

Whatever your circumstances, this book aims to help you to see more clearly how to tackle business writing effectively. There is no single magic formula. What makes a business technique work (though it may be based on certain fundamental approaches) is a matter of attention to a number of details. Certainly that is the case here.

COACH'S TIP

It is possible

You can write clearly and powerfully if you go about it in the right way and, if you do that, you will also begin to do it faster as well. In a busy life that is something worthwhile, too. But the primary step is to acknowledge that what you are currently doing can be changed.

WHAT IS IN IT FOR *YOU*?

Two questions no doubt arise as you begin this book:

- Am I going to learn anything new?
- If so, will it be useful?

This book not only presents a review of its topic and guidance about business writing, but also allows you, if you wish, to experiment and undertake a number of exercises and tasks – 'Coaching Sessions' – designed to help you absorb lessons and adopt the new practices more quickly and easily than otherwise might be the case.

In addition, each chapter contains the following features:

- **Outcomes**, which sets the theme for the chapter;

- **Coaching Sessions**, which vary in nature from simple exercises and thought-provokers to action designed to link to your own work and writing. In many of these it is suggested that you write in the space provided to complete the exercise or you may have a notebook by you as you go through the text;
- **Coach's Tips**, which emphasize key points;
- **Next Steps**, which preview the next chapter; and
- **Takeaways**, which form a summary and pose questions to further help you link this guide to real-life situations.

Towards the end of the book the **Quick Help** provides a summary of key issues, a final word and link to the future. It is followed by an **Action Plan** section to enable you to plan what action you may want to take next to ensure lessons get implemented and positively affect your work.

COACHING SESSION 1

The link to your own tasks

So, before we go any further, you may find it useful to think about what you have to write and assemble some examples from the past that you can refer to along the way.

Three tasks will enable you to have this ready as you then read on:

1. List the different types of document that you need (or will need) to write. If you write both long and short documents, be sure to include both.

2. Note, perhaps with an asterisk (*), those that are most important (either being most numerous or representing the greatest difficulty or opportunity).
3. Locate in your files a few typical documents, perhaps at least one long and one short, to keep with you and use as a guide to current practice as you proceed through the book. Note here what they are, for reference.

Note: While you are considering your own material, it will also be useful to identify a writing task, something real that you have to do in due course and which could perhaps be examined alongside your reading of this book.

NEXT STEPS

In this introduction you have:

- begun to focus on what makes business writing important, and what is likely to be difficult
- learned that good business writing is possible if you approach it in the right way and that old habits can be changed.

In the next chapter the dangers of bad business writing are explored more specifically, and ... we explore the way in which an appropriate focus on the needs of the reader can improve things.

TAKEAWAY

In this first introductory Takeaway, just two questions are posed. It may be useful to note your responses to both so that you can refer back during your ongoing reading.

1. Describe your attitude to the business writing you must do – do you see it as a, perhaps awkward, chore and if so why is this?

2. Look back at the examples of your own work that you selected in Coaching Session 1 and run a critical eye over them (briefly at this stage) but mark, perhaps in red, anything you feel is less clear than it might be – how would you rate them overall as pieces of writing (marks out of ten)?

2 THE DANGERS AND OPPORTUNITIES

OUTCOMES FROM THIS CHAPTER

- In this chapter we investigate the nature of business writing and the broad importance it has for us all in the workplace. We also highlight the fact that you need to be aware of the dangers inherent in poorly deployed writing – and the opportunities presented by the good.

The modern workplace is hectic and writing anything at all can seem a chore. There are surely more important things to be done - people to meet, decisions to be made, action to be taken. Yet all of these things and more can be dependent on written communication. A letter or memo may set up a meeting, a report may present a case and prompt a decision, and a proposal may act persuasively to ensure certain action is taken or a particular option is selected.

But *reading* business messages can be a chore also, and they will not achieve their purpose unless they are read, understood and do their job well enough to actively prompt the reader to action.

COACH'S TIP

You make it work

The first rule is to recognize the realities of how business writing is perceived and accept that it must earn a reading. You must make what you write deserve a reading.

COACHING SESSION 2

A bit of fun

That said, and the obvious conclusion is that you need an awareness of language to make it work. A little exercise makes this point. Take a moment to read the following paragraph and see if you can answer the question it poses.

'As you scan this short paragraph, try to spot what is unusual about it. Half an hour is normal for many to find a solution that is both logical and satisfactory to its originator. I do not say that anything is "wrong" about it, simply that it is unusual. You may want to study its grammatical construction to find a solution, but that is not a basis of its abnormality, nor is its lack of any information, logical points or conclusion. If you work in communications you may find that an aid to solving this particular conundrum. It is not about anagrams, synonyms, antonyms or acrostics, but it is unusual. So, why is that?'

This exercise can be regarded as a bit of fun. You don't need to crack the problem before you move on; in fact you may like to keep it at the back of your mind for a while. When you are ready, the answer is shown at the start of Chapter 10.

THE CHARACTERISTICS OF WRITTEN MESSAGES

Understanding exactly why anything is written is important. This may seem self-evident, yet many reports, for instance, are no more than something 'about their topic'. Their purpose, if they have one, is not clear. Without clear intentions the tendency is for the report to ramble, to go round and round and not come to any clear conclusion.

Why are you writing?

Documents may be written for many reasons. For example, they may intend to:

- inform
- motivate
- persuade
- explain
- create a dialogue
- prompt debate
- stimulate ideas
- change opinions
- build on prior contacts.

Often, more than one intention is aimed at, and different messages or emphasis for different people can add further complexity.

COACHING SESSION 3

Reasons for writing

Consider the reasons for written communication just itemized above, and list below those that are regularly a consideration for you, marking those that are of especial importance or that you feel currently present the greatest challenge.

Bearing the reader in mind

Consider the nature of the written word with your reader's hat on for a moment (you are probably both a reader and a writer of business documents). Do you read everything that crosses your desk? Do you read every word of the documents you do read? Do you read everything from the first word through in sequence, or do you dip into things? Almost certainly the answers make it clear that you do not treat all written material equally. Some documents are more likely to be read than others. Of course, some subjects demand your attention. Who ignores a personal note from the Managing Director? But the fact that some items have to be read often doesn't make their reading any easier or more pleasurable.

Good writing, which means, not least, something that is easy to read and understand, will always be likely to get more attention than sloppy writing. Yet we all know that current standards in this area are by no means universally good.

Why? Maybe the problem can be laid at the door of education, or more importantly the lack of it. Often, school (and sometimes even university) assists little with the kind of writing we find ourselves having to do once we are in the workplace.

Maybe it is a lack of feedback; perhaps managers are too tolerant of what is put in front of them. If more poor writing were rejected, and had to be rewritten, then more attention might be brought to bear on the task.

Habits are important here too. We all develop a style of writing and may find it difficult to shift away from it. Worse, bad habits may be reinforced by practice. For example, word-processing means that the ubiquitous standard document can often be used year after year with no one prepared to say 'scrap it', even if they notice how inadequate it has become.

BASIC PRINCIPLES

We can easily make fun of slips of the pen (or mind?). The UK Government's Environment Agency once announced that it had 'helped to make our environment a safer place by managing a UK scheme to dispose of surplus radioactive sources in schools, museums and hospitals'.

Are your kids glowing in the dark? Or is this piece somewhat badly worded?

We can learn more from the approach taken to writing, than from the one odd phrase. So at this stage, let's analyse writing through an example, and review a typical business letter.

COACHING SESSION 4

Analysis of writing

The example that follows is a real one, though the originator's name (one property of a major international hotel chain) has been removed. Usually addressed by name, and slipped under the door to greet us on the last day of a stay in a hotel, this is a typical business letter.

Dear Guest

We would like to thank you for allowing us to serve you here at the XXXX Hotel and hope that you are enjoying your stay.

Our records show that you are scheduled to depart today, and we wish to point out that our check-out time is 12 noon. Should you be departing on a later flight, please contact our front desk associates who will be happy to assist you with a late check-out. Also, please let us know if you require transport to the airport so that we can reserve one of our luxury Mercedes limousines.

In order to facilitate your check-out for today, we would like to take this opportunity to present you with a copy of your up-dated charges, so that you may review them at your convenience. Should you find any irregularities or have any questions regarding the attached charges, please do not hesitate to contact us.

We wish you a pleasant onward journey today, and hope to have the privilege of welcoming you back to the hotel again in the near future.

Sincerely yours,

(Name)

Front Office Manager

Before reading on, and bearing in mind what has been said so far, you might like to consider this example in some detail. Ask yourself what its purpose is and how well it achieves it. Check whether you understand it, and see if you find its tone – addressing a guest of a hospitality business – suitable, correct and easy to read. Make notes below of any comments you have, which you can refer back to later.

The process of analysing text is a practical one. It may be useful to read the comments about this example that follow, then return and spend a little longer analysing something else (e.g. a letter you have written or received).

Observations on the example

What are we to make of such a letter? It is, necessarily, a standard one used many times each day. It came to my notice when it was slipped under my door, and taking note of the bit about late check-outs, '...will be happy to assist you...', I went to Reception to take advantage of the offer. Not only was I told, 'Sorry, we're too full to do that today', so were a dozen *other* people during the ten minutes I was standing at the desk.

So, the first conclusion is that the letter is so badly expressed that it does more harm than good, causing as much disappointment as satisfaction because it says clearly that something will happen when it should really be saying something may only *sometimes* be possible.

It is also very old fashioned, with rather pompous sounding phrases such as: '... we wish to point out that...' and '...we would like to take this opportunity...', when something shorter, more straightforward and business-like would surely be better.

It almost suggests that the account may potentially be wrong ('irregularities'), and everything is expressed from an introspective point of view: 'We', 'we' and 'we' again leading into almost every point. No, it is not good and your own analysis may well run longer.

At its core, the essential problem is perhaps intention. What has the letter been designed to do? To...:

- simply remind people to pay the bill?
- make check-out quicker or easier?
- sell a transport service to the airport?
- persuade people to come and stay again (presumably by giving an impression of efficiency and good service)?
- just say 'Thank you'.

Because it mixes up all of these to some extent, it fails to do justice to any of them. For example, nothing about the check-out procedure is explained, nor are compelling reasons given as to why someone should stay again. Yet this should surely be straightforward; perhaps that is why it was given inadequate thought.

As well as making an immediate point about the care needed when using standard letters – use them by all means, but make sure they are good – it leads neatly to the next point.

MESSAGES ARE FRAGILE

All of us can readily recognize a really bad document, without structure or style but with an excess of jargon, convoluted sentences and which has readers thinking: 'What is this trying to say?' But such documents do not have to be a *complete* mess to fail in their purpose. Messages are inherently fragile. One wrongly chosen word may dilute understanding or damage what would otherwise be a positive impression.

Even something as simple as a spelling mistake, and computer spell chequers (sic) are fallible, may have a negative effect.

I will never forget, in my first year in a consulting firm, playing a small part in proposals that were submitted to a dairy products company. After meetings, deliberations and then more meetings, a written proposal was sent. A week passed. Then an envelope arrived from the company concerned. Inside was a single sheet of paper. It was a copy of the title page of the proposal and on it was written, in red ink, the three words 'No thank you' alongside a red ring drawn around one typed word. The word 'Dairy' in the company's name had been spelled 'Diary'. For a long while after that everything was checked very much more carefully. The implication is clear.

The very first rule to drum into your mind should be 'check, check and check again'. Mistakes that remind us to do so are often on public display (like the rather surreal one I saw recently in a lift that said 'Only use the buttons provided').

Whether you are guilty of a major or minor error the potential for damage is the same. So obviously, the quality of writing matters.

SIGNIFICANT OPPORTUNITY

Suffice it to say that should prevailing writing standards remain low, then there is a major opportunity for those who outperform that standard. More so for those who excel. Never forget the permanence of the written word – your bad documents might just come back to haunt you.

So, effective business writing is a vital skill. There may be a great deal hanging on a document doing the job it is intended to do – accurate action, a decision, a sale, a financial result or a personal reputation. Very real opportunities exist for those who can acquire sound skills in this area. The more you write, and the more important the documents you create, the truer this is. Quite simply, if you write well then you are more likely to achieve your business goals.

This point cannot be overemphasized. One sheet of paper may not change the world, but well written – it can be influential and effectual.

We may not all aspire to or succeed in writing the great novel (mine is still to be published!), but most people can learn to turn out good business writing. Writing that is well tailored to its purpose and likely to create the effect that was intended.

Good business writing need not be difficult. It is a skill, certainly, but one that can be developed with study and practice. Some effort may be involved, and practice undeniably helps. According to William Somerset Maugham: 'There are three rules for writing the novel. Unfortunately, no one knows what they are.'

Business writing is not so dependent on creativity, though it is involved, and it is subject to certain rules. Rules, of course, are made to be broken. But they can act as useful guidelines and therefore be a help. More of rules anon...

COMMUNICATION HAZARDS

Documentation is essentially only a form of communication and however a message is put over, even if there is no paper (as with something sent through email, for example), it has to be composed in some way.

Any organization would be stifled with no communication; indeed, nothing much would happen. Communication – good communication – should oil the wheels of organizational activity and facilitate action. This is true of even the simplest memo, and is certainly so of something longer and more complex like a report.

Communication is – inherently – inclined to be less than straightforward. If this is true for snippets of information, how greater the potential for misunderstanding does a 25-page report present? And with written communication the danger is that any confusion lasts. There is not necessarily an immediate opportunity for the reader to check (the writer might be 100 miles away), and a misunderstanding on page 3 may skew the whole message and negate the purpose of an entire report.

ERRORS APLENTY

Once something has been written, any error that causes misunderstanding is made permanent. The dangers of ill-thought-out writing are various. Such writing may:

- be wrong, but still manage to convey its meaning, like the cookery book that advises: 'To stop your eyes watering when chopping onions, put them in the freezer.' Or the Air New Zealand advertisement that offered 'Round the world tickets from £698 return'. There is something worrying about the thought of a round-the-world trip that doesn't return you to your starting point.

  Such things may amuse but will probably be understood. No great harm done, perhaps, though the first example might just throw doubt on the credibility of the recipe as a whole. Indeed, any fault tends to highlight the possibility of other, more serious, problems.

- try too hard to please, ending up giving the wrong impression. In one Renaissance Hotel there are signs on the coffee shop tables that say: 'COURTESY OF CHOICE: The concept and symbol of "Courtesy of Choice" reflect the centuries-old philosophy that acknowledges differences while allowing them to exist together in harmony. "Courtesy of Choice" accommodates the preferences of individuals by offering both smoking and non-smoking areas in the spirit of conviviality and mutual respect.' An absurd over-politeness just ends up making the message sound rude – this restaurant has both smoking and non-smoking areas and seems to be saying if you find yourself next to a smoker, then tough. This kind of thing does matter.

- be incomprehensible. A press release is an important piece of writing. One, quoted in the national press, was sent out by the consulting group Accenture. The item commented that Accenture envisioned 'a world where economic activity is ubiquitous, unbounded by the traditional definitions of commerce and universal'. Err, yes – or rather, no. The newspaper referred not to the content of the release, only to the fact that it contained a statement so wholly gobbledygook as to have no meaning at all. It is sad when any writing is so bad that it fails to achieve anything at all.
- be nonsense. A cooker advertisement says Neff's CircoSteam doesn't have complicated functions – just simple one-touch controls, including 52 cooking programmes (and that's simple?).

And be careful if all this gives you a headache: one pack of pills suggests that you 'swallow with a glass full of water'. A glassful is less likely to stick in your throat!

COACHING SESSION 5

Critiquing your work

See if you can find similar errors in your example exhibits (yours, or material you routinely see), using the headings below; that is, things that are:

1. Wrong

____

____

____

____

____

____

____

____

____

____

2. Trying too hard to please

3. Incomprehensible

4. Nonsense

You could doubtless extend such a list of examples extensively. The point here is clear: it is all too easy for the written word to fail. All of the above were probably the subject of some thought and checking but clearly not enough. Put pen to paper and you step onto dangerous ground.

So, the first requirement of good business writing is clarity. Think of how regularly you are faced with brief email messages and, because they are ambiguous in some way, you simply have to reply asking for clarification. Much time is wasted this way. Similarly, composing a good report needs thinking about if it is to be clear, and it should never be taken for granted that what we write will be clearly understood.

It is more likely that we will give due consideration to clarity, and give it the attention it needs, if we are clear about the purpose of any document.

YOUR READERS' EXPECTATIONS

For a document to be well received, it must meet certain expectations of its readers. Before going into these, let us consider generally what conditions such expectations. Psychologists talk about what they call 'cognitive cost'.

There is no better example than to remember the 1980s video recorder. If you wanted to do something other than the basics, you needed to get out the instruction book. Big mistake! You opened it and any two-page spread shouted at you 'This is going to be difficult!'

Such a document has what is called a 'high cognitive cost' (that is, the cost in time and aggravation of understanding something), rather than appearing inviting. Even a cursory look may be offputting. Such documents have improved (or maybe the technology has got easier!) but you might have similar current examples that come to mind as examples of baffling writing.

People are wary of this effect. They may even look at documents expecting them to be hard work. If they then discover it looks easier and more inviting than they first thought (a 'low cognitive cost'), then they are likely to read them with more enthusiasm. But what gives people the feeling, both at first glance and as they delve further into it, that a document should not be avoided on principle?

COACHING SESSION 6

As a reader

Consider the following with your reader's hat on. List, in a word or two, the overall characteristics that you hope a document that you have to read will exhibit (we will come to specific details of language later).

1.

2.

3.

4.

5.

6.

7.

8.

9.

10.

The following lists some of the key factors that readers prefer. People like it – and are more likely to give something their attention – if a document is:

- **brief:** Obviously a shorter document is likely to be easier to read than something longer, but what really matters is that any document is of an appropriate length for its topic and purpose. Perhaps the best word to apply is succinct – 'to the point'. A report may be 10 pages long, or 50, and still qualify for this description
- **succinct:** This makes clear that length is inextricably linked to message. If there is a rule, then it is to make something long enough to carry the message – then stop
- **relevant:** Cover what is required, without irrelevant content or digression
- **clear:** Readers must be able to understand it. And this applies in numerous ways. For example, it should be clearly written (in the sense of not being convoluted) and use appropriate language. You should not feel that, as an intended reader, you have to look up every other word in a dictionary
- **precise:** Saying *exactly* what is necessary
- **in 'our language':** In other words, using a tone and style of language that is likely to make sense to the average (or intended) reader, and which displays evidence of being designed to do so
- **simple:** Avoiding unnecessary complexity (more of this anon)
- **well structured:** So that it proceeds logically through a sequence that is clear and appears to be a sensible way of dealing with the message. It may be useful to both describe the structure used and explain why it is appropriate to readers
- **descriptive:** Again we will return to this later, but here it is enough to say that if there is a need to paint a picture it must be done so in a way that creates a clear image.

COACH'S TIP

Comprehensiveness

Never consider comprehensiveness to be an objective. If a report, say, touched on everything possible (i.e. comprehensive) then it would certainly be too long. In fact, you always have to be selective, and make good content choices.

Whether writing for an internal (a colleague perhaps) or external audience, you need to be clear about what your communications seek to achieve and what kinds of expectations exist for them at the other end.

For example, a technical person may have different expectations from a lay person, and may be looking to check a level of detail that must exist and be clearly expressed for a document to be acceptable to them. Always focus on your recipients in this way as you write.

Focus on the readers' perspective

So, logically from what has already been said in this chapter, it is clear that good business writing must reflect the needs of the reader. Such writing cannot be undertaken in a vacuum. It is not simply an opportunity for the writer to say the things he or she wants to. Ultimately, only an audience can judge whether a document is any good.

An eye on the reader

Your readers' perspective is the starting point and throughout the writing process you need to think about who your intended readers are, how they think, how they view the topic that you are writing about, what their experience to date is of the issues, and how they are likely to react to what you have to say.

THE POWER OF HABITS

Habit, and the ongoing pressure of work, can combine to push people into writing on 'automatic pilot'. Sometimes, if you critique something that you wrote, or that went out from your department, you can clearly see something that is wrong. A sentence that does not make sense, a point that fails to get across or a description that confuses rather than clarifies.

Usually the reason this has occurred is not that the writer really thought this was the best sentence or phrase to use, and then got it wrong. Rather it was because there was inadequate thought of any sort, or none at all.

Habits can be difficult to break and the end result can be a plethora of material circulating around organizations couched in a kind of gobbledygook or what some call 'officespeak'.

Earning a reading

The moral here is clear. Good writing does not just happen. It needs some thought and some effort (and some study, with which this book aims to assist). The process needs to be actively worked at if the result is going to do the job you have in mind.

COACH'S TIP

Get into the habit

Remember that good habits can be just as powerful as bad ones. A shift of emphasis from one to the other is possible and the rewards of so doing make the 'game very much worth the candle'.

WHAT CAN BE ACHIEVED

Think about what good writing skills can achieve. Consider the example of reports; they can influence action. But they can also reveal an image of the writer.

Within an organization of any size, people interact through communication. They send each other emails, they sit in meetings and on committees, they chat as they pass on the stairs, or share a sandwich at lunchtime and everything about the way they do all this sends out signals. It tells the world, or at least the rest of the organization, something about them. Are they knowledgeable, competent, expert, decisive and easy to deal with – would you take their advice, follow their lead or support their cause?

All the different ways in which people interrelate act together, cumulatively and progressively, to build and maintain an image of each individual. Some ways may play a disproportionate part, and business writing is such an example. There are two reasons why this effect is important:

- All documents, unlike more transient means of communication, can last. They are passed around, considered and may well remain on the record; more so if they are about important issues.
- Because not everyone can write effectively, people can be impressed by a clear ability to marshal an argument and put it over in writing.

Thus business writing represents an opportunity – or rather two opportunities.

Business writing – at least when it is good – can be instrumental in prompting action. The kind of action you want. It is also important to your profile. What you write says something about the kind of person you are, how effective you are and what it is like to work with you. In a sense there are situations where you want to make sure that certain personal qualities shine through. For example, a case may be supported by it being clear that the person who is presenting it has provided plenty of attention to detail.

Longer term, the view taken of someone by their bosses may be influenced by their regularly reading of what they regard as good reports. So, next time you are burning the midnight oil to get some seemingly tedious report finalized, think of it as the business equivalent of an open goal and remember that it could be affecting your chances of promotion!

Achieving your aims

Many business documents demand detailed work. Their preparation may, on occasion, seem tedious. They certainly need adequate time set aside for them. But as the old saying has it: 'If a job is worth doing, it is worth doing well.' It may take no more time to write effectively than it does to do so in a lacklustre way. This is true for reports, emails or for any other document. The next chapter contends that a systematic approach can even speed up your writing.

If whatever you write is clear, focused and set out so as to earn a reading, then you are more likely to achieve your purpose. In this case, too, good writing is also more likely to act positively to enhance the profile of the writer. Both these results are surely worthwhile?

But the job still has to be done, the words still have to be got down on paper, and faced with a blank sheet of paper (or, nowadays, a computer screen) this can be a daunting. Go about it in the right way, however, and it does become possible.

NEXT STEPS

This chapter has set the scene in terms of the dangers of poor writing and the opportunities that make it worthwhile to learn to execute it well. The following should be noted particularly:

- Remember that communication has inherent dangers; clear communication needs to be well considered
- Your messages will only achieve their purpose if you are clear in your mind what you are seeking to achieve
- The reader is more important than the writer; write for others, not for yourself
- Beware old habits (that serve you ill) and work to establish good new ones
- What you write has the potential to be a powerful tool – powerful in action terms, and powerful in contributing to your personal profile.

The next chapter turns to the actual mechanics of getting the words down and what makes it possible to do so effectively.

TAKEAWAY

This section is designed to give you a moment to take stock. You may decide to read on, return to earlier coaching sessions or make some notes of your progress to date and factors likely to be important to you in the future. Some notes in response to the questions here may prove useful as you proceed.

What dangers are most likely givetn the nature of the kinds of things you most usually write about?

Can you recall any recent stand-out errors of phraseology in your own writing, or that of colleagues?

Given the importance of checking to achieving an effective document, are you always sufficiently thorough, and, if not, are there any bad habits you should change or good habits to add to ensure you can answer affirmatively in future?

How will reading your documents (in whole or part) affect readers in terms of change?

3 GETTING THE RIGHT WORDS DOWN

OUTCOMES FROM THIS CHAPTER

- This chapter will show you how to approach the actual job of setting the words down, first by exploring what the objectives are for any particular document. It then promotes the benefits of a systematic approach towards writing and how so doing helps you achieve what you want.

In the interests of taking one thing at a time, we'll leave the essentials of language and writing style to one side (for now) and, perhaps with the words of William Somerset Maugham in mind – 'All the words I use... can be found in a dictionary – it's just a matter of arranging them into the right sentences' – we look next at how you get set to write something in a way that will be likely to make it effective, and specifically at how you start the actual process of writing.

COACHING SESSION 7

Now write...

Before you read any further you should practise by writing something. There are two stages to this exercise.

1. Ideally, pick something real to you that will be about a page in extent. (Or, if you want an example, an easy-to-follow suggestion appears below.) Take a sheet of paper or sit at a blank computer screen and, allowing yourself ten minutes to do so, start to write on that topic. But... hang on... I want you to pause after five minutes.

Example suggestion: Here's something that you can pitch into quickly and easily. Imagine that you have to write something about your job. To make it more interesting, and to give it a specific objective, imagine that you are writing a letter designed to attract internal candidates to apply for your job, since you are to be promoted once a successful applicant has been found.

2. Now consider, not so much what you have written (which, if you used the example above, may have touched on a variety of aspects of the job from salary to objectives,

training to qualifications and experience needed), but how you are *actually* going about writing it. For example, ask yourself:

- What were you going to write next?
- What was to be the final point you would make?
- Did you, in fact, have a plan and if so was it detailed enough?
- If not, or if it was inadequate, consider how it may have helped.

There is space below to makes some notes from the experience and how you have thought about it.

Note: In tackling Coaching Session 7 you would not be unusual if you just plunged in and pretty much just started writing with no real plan or at least a very thin one.

Furthermore, knowing you have to write something (especially something long) can prompt different responses in different people: you may put it off, doodle or write some central part quickly and ahead of the rest 'because you know that bit'. Whatever your current writing habits and practices are, you might want to consider the exercise below before continuing with this chapter.

COACHING SESSION 8

The 'how' of your writing

There was no need to complete the writing in the exercise above, but it might be useful, at this point, to have something that you have written beside you as you read on, and to think particularly about how it was written – what procedure and actions, in what order, went into drafting it.

You can do this quickly by locating something (preferably recent, so that you still have the details of it in mind) from your own material assembled earlier, or from your files, and make some notes here as to how you composed it.

There will probably be bad habits you identify and want to make a mental note to drop, things not done that you now feel would be useful, and hopefully some things you want to retain. Make notes below:

1. Bad methods to drop:

2. Good methods to introduce:

3. Useful methods to retain:

ENGAGE BRAIN BEFORE WRITING

Rarely can areas of business skill be acquired instantly through some magic formula, and business writing is no exception. However, preparation perhaps comes close to acting in this way. It really is the foundation upon which successful writing is based. Preparation allows you to do two things.

First, to create a document that you not only feel content with, but one that has a clear purpose and that is regarded as useful by its readers. As has been said previously, the ultimate measure of good business writing is whether it achieves the outcome you wish.

Secondly, a systematic approach to preparation and writing will save you time. This is a worthy result in its own right. Which of us does not have too much to do?

When I first had to do a significant amount of writing, and therefore needed to look into what made it work well in order to improve my own practices, I found that the way I worked did change. It was a surprise that in addition to the effect it may have had on the quality of what I wrote, I was also getting my writing done more quickly.

This experience has been echoed by the many people I have met through conducting training on this topic and is, I suspect, something you will find too. Perhaps it was ever thus: Roman rhetorician Quintilian opined – 'Write quickly, and you will never write well; write well, and you will soon write quickly.'

Next, therefore, we'll review the actual process of preparation and getting the words down, starting with what you should not do. Do **not** start, faced with the task of writing a 20-page report, say, by getting out a clean sheet of paper and immediately writing: '1. INTRODUCTION. This report sets out ....'.

As we have already seen, thinking **must** precede writing. In other words, you need to engage the brain before your hands. Yet many people start all their writing this way: they start writing and planning together (as you may have seen in Coaching Session 7).

Ask: what must my writing achieve?

In common with much else, any business document – even a short email – needs clear objectives. Let's be specific: objectives are not what you wish to *say*, they are what you wish to *achieve*. Put simply, the task is not to write, say, 'about the new policy'; rather it is to ensure people understand a proposed change and how it is intended to work. This in turn is designed to ensure people accept the necessity for it and are prompted to undertake their future work in a way that fits with the new policy.

With this kind of clarity of intention the writing is already likely to be easier. With a more specific situation in mind (perhaps the 'your job' topic described earlier), objectives can be formed precisely if, as the oft-quoted acronym has it, they are SMART. That is:

- Specific
- Measurable
- Achievable
- Realistic
- Timed.

To illustrate this principle, imagine you are setting up a training course on the subject of, say, report writing. What objectives would you set? Following the SMART principles the course should:

- enable participants to create future reports that are written in a way that will be seen by their readers as appropriate, informative and, above all, readable (specific)
- ensure action occurs after the session (measurable) – e.g. future proposals might be measured by the number of recipients who subsequently confirmed agreement
- be appropriate for the chosen group – e.g. an inexperienced group might need a longer and more detailed programme than one formed by people with more experience – and thus have achievable objectives
- be not just achievable but realistic – e.g. the time away from the job should be balanced with the potential results springing from the course to ensure attendance was desirable
- be timed – e.g. when is the workshop? In a month's time or in six months? And how long will it last? 1 day? 2 days? Results cannot come until it has taken place.

COACH'S TIP

Bearing the reader in mind

Objectives should be phrased more in terms of readers rather than the writer. Overall the following two key questions must be answered clearly:

- **Why** am I writing this?
- **What** am I trying to achieve?

COACHING SESSION 9

Clear objectives

Now return to the example you used in Coaching Session 7. Start again from scratch and create and note clear objectives for the document (using the SMART formula).

COACH'S TIP

Ensuring complete statements of intent

To check whether an answer to either of the questions in the last 'Tip' is too vague to be useful, ask of it 'which means that…' and see if this leads to a more specific statement. For example, you might say that such a course is designed to 'improve writing skills'. So far so good, but what does this mean exactly? It means that documents will be less time consuming to prepare than in the past, more reader-oriented and more likely to achieve their objectives. This way of thinking can be pursued until objectives are absolutely specific and clear.

Be clear

Never put 'pen to paper' until you are clear in your mind what objectives you are addressing. Once your objectives are set satisfactorily you can proceed to the real business of getting something down on paper, though this still does not mean starting at the beginning and writing on to the end.

A SYSTEMATIC APPROACH

Not many people can write at length without making a few notes first, and frankly the complexity of many documents often demands a little more than this. Sometimes all that is needed is a dozen words on the back of the proverbial envelope, but you need to be very sure that you are not missing anything. Unless you are thoroughly prepared, the chances are that whatever you create as your first draft will be somewhat off-target, and time must then be spent tinkering and reworking to get it into order. Typically, this takes more time than if prior thought had been given at the outset.

Another danger is time. Writing may fail only because it is rushed (and therefore thinking time is insufficient). Or time problems are compounded by deadlines. And who has never had to work to tighter deadlines than they would like? Too often skimping preparation, combined with a pressing deadline, means that something must be submitted even though the writer knows that an additional review and some more editing would make it more likely to do its job well.

A seven-stage approach

So, to encompass all possibilities and degrees of complexity, the following seven-stage approach sets out a methodology that will cope with any kind of document, short or long (it is the way this book began life too).

It is recommended because it works. It will make the job quicker and the conclusion more certain. It can instil the right habits and rapidly becomes something you can work with, utilizing its methods more or less comprehensively depending on the circumstances.

COACHING SESSION 10

Your systematic approach

In order to apply the methodology described here, you could usefully return to your own examples and select a recently written piece (or take something you have to write soon and prepare to write it going through the seven steps as you feel appropriate and necessary).

Note: Two methods are suggested for doing this; whichever suits you better will depend on your inclination and the nature of the example you take. You can either:

- Pause after each of the seven stages and work on that linking it to your example, or
- Wait until you have read through the seven stages and then work on the exercise as a whole.

Some space is allowed on this page, but it may in fact be better at this point to do the work on a separate sheet of paper and/or computer screen.

The stages are now reviewed in turn. As mentioned earlier, you may want to follow this with a specific example in mind.

The following methodology provides a pathway. You can follow it or adapt it. You can pare it down somewhat for straightforward documents, but not too much – omitting significant elements of the different stages can make writing slower, more awkward and mean the end result is less good than would otherwise be the case.

Stage 1: Research

Research may or may not be necessary. It may be that everything you need is in your head. More likely, you may need to do some digging, or at least some assembling.

For example, let us suppose you are writing about one of your company's products. It may make sense to gather together previous documents describing it, technical literature, even the product itself, and have these to hand as you commence the job. It may be that you need to cast the net wider; in this case, what about the competition's product material, for example? Similarly, to create continuity, if writing something like a newsletter, you would sensibly have any earlier issues to hand.

No hard and fast rule applies here. You should, however, ask yourself what might be useful and take a moment to collect and look at or read what the task suggests is necessary.

Note: Depending on how you wish to proceed, you may turn to Coaching Session 10 here.

Stage 2: List the contents

Next, with your objective in mind but ignoring just for the moment sequence, structure and arrangement, just list – in short note (or keyword) form – every significant point you might want to make. Give yourself plenty of space; certainly use one side of paper as it lets you see everything at a glance without turning over. List the points as they occur to you, randomly across the page.

You will find that this process (which is akin to mind-mapping) acts as a good thought prompter. It enables you to fill out a picture as one thing leads to another, with the freestyle approach removing the need to think or worry about anything else, even how to link the points together. The scale of this stage may vary. It may be as few as six words on the back of an envelope, or generally be somewhat more expansive on an A4 sheet (this book started life on a sheet of flipchart paper divided into squares for the chapters).

Note: Depending on how you wish to proceed, you may turn to Coaching Session 10 here.

Stage 3: Sorting it out

That done, you can bring some sort of order to bear. Review what you have noted down and decide on:

- the sequence in which points should go
- which points link logically
- what is ancillary, providing illustration, evidence or example to exemplify points made
- whether the list is complete (you may continue to think of things to add), or whether some things on it can be omitted without weakening the overall message. This final point links to careful consideration of length; clearly most documents need to be contained to some degree.

The quickest and easiest way to undertake this stage is simply to annotate your original workings by highlighting and amending them in a second colour. This is for your reference only; you may find it helpful to use arrows, or to circle words or draw symbols or pictures.

Note: Depending on how you wish to proceed, you may turn to Coaching Session 10 here.

Stage 4: Arrange the content

Sometimes at the end of the previous stage you have a picture/plan that you can follow and no more needs to be done. Often, however, what you have in front of you can be a bit of a colourful mess. By arranging it I mean simply turning it into a neat listing; this could also be the stage at which you type it out to finish the job on screen. Most people seem to input their own written material nowadays (I sometimes think the typing is harder work than the writing!).

Final revision is, of course, still possible at this stage but when that's done (and it might include getting another opinion about it from, say, a colleague) you are left with a clear list that sets out the content, sequence and emphasis to whatever level of detail you find helpful. Some experimentation may be useful here; certainly I am not suggesting that you over-engineer the process. This sheet then becomes your blueprint from which you write. You must decide the form in which this is most useful.

Note: Depending on how you wish to proceed, you may turn to Coaching Session 10 here.

Stage 5: A final review

This may not always be necessary – or possible (deadlines may be looming) – but it can be useful to leave it a while – sleep on it – and only start writing after you come back to it afresh. You can get very close to things, and it helps you to see it more clearly if you step back and distract your mind with something else for a while.

Now, with a final version of what is effectively your writing plan in front of you, you can – at last – actually start to draft the text.

Note: Depending on how you wish to proceed, you may turn to Coaching Session 10 here.

Stage 6: Writing

Now you write or type or dictate the words you feel best carry your message. This is where the real work is, though it is very much easier with a clear plan for the task.

What you have done here is obvious, but significant. You have separated the two tasks: one of deciding what to write, the other of deciding how to put it. Being a bear of very little brain I for one certainly find this easier; so too do many other people. This is one of the most useful results of the approach described here and allows more thought to be applied, logically and easily, to both aspects of the writing.

As will be clear in the next chapter, when you think about how to put things, the language issues do demand some consideration.

Note: Depending on how you wish to proceed, you may turn to Coaching Session 10 here.

So now you have a draft, though already you may feel that it needs further work. Now what?

COACH'S TIP

Choose the right moment

If possible, pick a time to write when you are 'in the mood'. There seem to be times when words flow more easily than others. Also, interruptions can disrupt the flow and make writing take much longer as you recap in your mind, get back into something and continue. It is not always possible, of course, but a bit of organization to get as close as possible to the 'non-interruption' ideal is very worthwhile.

COACH'S TIP

Keep writing

Do not stop and agonize over small details. If you cannot think of the right word, a suitable heading – whatever – put in a row of 'xxxxxx's and continue; you can always return and fill in such gaps later, but if you lose the whole thread and your train of thought, then writing becomes more difficult and will take longer to do. Again the idea of preserving the flow in this way can quickly become a habit, especially once you are convinced it helps.

Stage 7: Editing

Few – if any – people write perfect copy first time and alter nothing. If you write, then some editing goes with the territory. So, rule one is not to feel inadequate, but to accept that this is the way it works and allow a little time for revision.

Careful preparation, as suggested in earlier stages, should minimize the need for alterations; at least you should not be finding things you have left out or altering the whole structure. The words may need work, however. Computer spelling and grammar checkers are very useful. But be warned, not every spelling inaccuracy is corrected (for example, homophones such as 'their', 'there' and 'they're' will not be detected); proper names and such like may need care, too. Grammar checkers should not be followed slavishly, especially for the punchy style you need for some business messages.

Perhaps a sensible rule here is not to ignore anything highlighted as grammatically incorrect, unless you can give yourself a good reason for so doing.

COACH'S TIP

Making editing work

Improve the effectiveness of your editing by:

- sleeping on it: since distance lends clarity
- getting a colleague to check it: maybe you can do a swap with someone else who would value you looking at some of their written material – it is amazing how a fresh eye and brain picks up things to which you are, or have become, blind. Incidentally, listen to what they say and consider it carefully; it is easy to become automatically defensive and reject what, with hindsight, may turn out to be good advice
- being thorough: do not regard editing as a chore; it is an inherent part of getting writing right!

Editing is an important stage. Seemingly small changes such as substituting a word, breaking an overlong sentence into two, adding more and better placed punctuation, all may make a real difference. This is the time to bear in mind style and use of language (see next chapter) as well as sense and clarity. Then when you are happy with it, let it go: press 'print' or whatever comes next.

It is easy to tinker forever. You will always think of something else that could be put differently (better?) if you leave it and look again; but productivity and deadlines are important too

Note: Depending on how you wish to proceed, you may turn to Coaching Session 10 here.

Ensure that your version of this systematic approach becomes a habit and you will find that your writing improves, and that writing actually gets easier. As a rule of thumb, set aside a proportion of the total time you allocate, or simply need, for writing for preparation. If you find that say 15–30 per cent of the time, or whatever works for you, is necessary, you will also find that rather than 'additional' preparation increasing the overall task time, such jobs actually begin to take less time.

Simply pitching in and starting immediately at the top of a blank sheet of paper (or computer screen) with no preparation is not the quicker option that perhaps it sometimes seems to be.

If you are conscious of how you write and think about what makes the writing process easier or more difficult for you, then you will no doubt add to this list and adopt further ways that help you. Of course, at the same time we must be realistic. There are things that interfere with how you would like to write, including deadlines that prohibit putting it off and other priorities and interruptions.

COACH'S TIP

Adopt the right attitude

In two ways:

- Do not let perfection be the enemy of the good; in other words, get as close as you can to your ideal way of operating, but do not let problems make you see the whole thing as impossible and abandon your good intentions entirely
- Use good habits to build up greater writing strength; for instance persevering with something until you *make it work for you*.

As an example of building habits, I used to be rather poor at writing on the move, but a busy life and regular travel made it necessary. Nowadays, after some perseverance, I can tune out the hustle and bustle of, say, a busy airport and get a good amount done.

A systematic approach really is half the battle; try it.

COACHING SESSION 10 (AGAIN)

You may have been working on this progressively, but if not you may want to tackle this now. The details of what to do are repeated here.

In order to apply the methodology described here, you could usefully return to your own examples and select a recently written piece (or take something you have to write soon) and prepare to write it going through the seven steps as you feel appropriate and necessary.

Some space is allowed on the page, but it may in fact be better at this point to do the work on a sheet of full-sized paper and/or computer screen.

ONLINE RESOURCE

Composition template

To allow you to follow the suggested systematic approach to writing, use a template/stepthru guide as you write a real document. The one here is designed to allow you to practise your technique, but could be of ongoing use for the most complex documents to ensure you keep on track.

www.TYCoachbooks.com/BusinessWriting

ONLINE RESOURCE

Composition template (exercise)

If you feel it would be useful to experiment and practise with this systematic approach, use an exercise and a topic prescribed by this exercise.

www.TYCoachbooks.com/BusinessWriting

NEXT STEPS

In this chapter the key lessons have been to:

- set a clear objective up front
- go about the task of writing systematically
- create and work to a writing plan
- fix on an approach that suits you and stick with it, creating useful individual habits in the process
- give the task space and priority
- check, check and cheque (sic) again
- separate deciding what you are going to include (content), from how you are going to express it (style), thus giving yourself two separate but complementary tasks rather than one more complex one.

We now pick up the second aspect of the last point – how you actually express things – and in the next chapter we review the use of language and how that contributes to clarity and your ability to achieve what you want.

This section is designed to give you a moment to take stock. You may decide to read on, return to earlier coaching sessions or make some notes of progress to date and factors likely to be important to you in the future. Some notes in response to the questions here may prove useful as you proceed.

Look at one of your own examples: is a clear objective evident, if not what should it have been?

Is the objective SMART (and thus sufficiently explicit)?

If you now regard your past planning to write stage insufficient, what steps can you take to experiment with a more thorough way and make that a good habit?

Editing is important and must be preceded by a thorough read through: is there a colleague who could help with this; if so, how might you broach an arrangement?

4 LANGUAGE TO CREATE EFFECTIVENESS

OUTCOMES FROM THIS CHAPTER

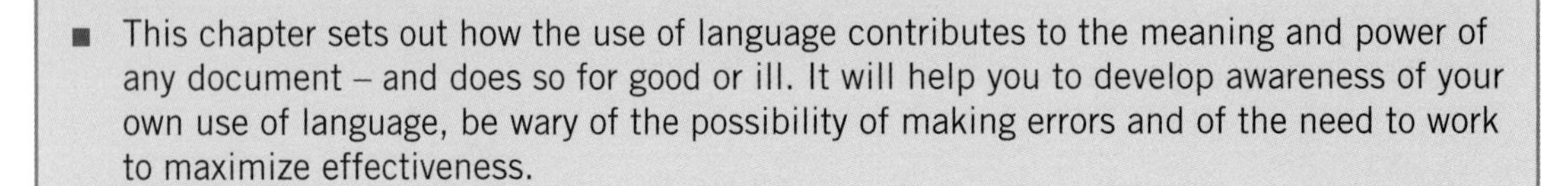

- This chapter sets out how the use of language contributes to the meaning and power of any document – and does so for good or ill. It will help you to develop awareness of your own use of language, be wary of the possibility of making errors and of the need to work to maximize effectiveness.

We are lucky that English is such a powerful language. Its vast vocabulary allows precise description. However, its oddball nature can make for some difficulty. For example, consider spelling, which can often seem awkward (irresistible is a commonly misspelled word); words (even simple ones: do you lie down, or lay down?); and the generally perverse nature of the way it sometimes works.

We can wonder about why the plural form of 'moose' isn't 'meese' when the plural of 'goose' is 'geese', why a wise man and a wise guy are opposites and why abbreviation is such a long word. No wonder writing can be difficult.

Words do matter, and so too do many other things about language. The precision with which you use it can make or break even a simple, written message. In Lewis Carroll's *Through the Looking Glass* Humpty Dumpty emphatically says: 'When I use a word, it means what I choose it to mean – neither more nor less', but realistically it is what your readers understand that matters.

THE WRITING PROCESS: WHAT TO SAY AND HOW TO SAY IT

How to start?

If you undertake to engender a totality of meaning which corresponds with the cognition of others seeking to intake a communication from the content you display in a report there is a greater likelihood of subsequent action being that which you desire.

You are correct. That is not a good start. If I want to say 'If you write well, people will understand and be more likely to react as you wish', then I should say just that. But the preceding convoluted sentence makes a good point with which to start this chapter.

Both language and how you use it matter. Exactly how you express things has a direct bearing on how they are received; and that in turn has a direct bearing on how well a document succeeds in its objectives.

It is clear language that makes a difference. But this is a serious understatement; language can make a very considerable difference. And it can make a difference in many different ways, as this chapter will show.

How you write must stem as much as anything from the view your intended readers have of what they want to read. Or in some cases are prepared to read, because – be honest – reading many business documents can be something of a chore. Perhaps this even applies to some you write!

Consider the following four broad elements. Readers want documents to be understandable, readable, straightforward and natural.

CREATE UNDERSTANDING

Clarity has been mentioned already. Its necessity may seem to go without saying, but it is all too easy to find everyday examples of wording that is less than clear. A favourite of mine is an odd sign you see from time to time: 'Ears pierced, while you wait.' There is some other way, perhaps? Maybe there has been a new technological development of which I am unaware.

Clarity is assisted by many of the elements mentioned in this chapter, but three factors help immensely:

- Using the right words: for example, are you writing about 'recommendations' or 'options', about 'objectives' (desired results) or 'strategies' (routes to achieving objectives), and when do you use 'aims' rather than 'goals'?
- Using the right phrases: what is '24-hour service' exactly?, other than not sufficiently specific. Ditto 'personal service'? Is this just saying it is done by people? If so it is hardly a glimpse of anything but the obvious; perhaps it needs expanding to explain the nature, and perhaps excellence, of the particular service approach.
- Selecting and arranging words to ensure that your meaning is clear: for example, saying – 'At this stage, the arrangement is...' implies that later on it will be something else (possibly not what was intended!). Saying: 'After working late into the night, the report will be with you this afternoon' seems to imply (because of the sequence and arrangement of words...) that it is the report (not the writer) that was working late.

Even changing a word or two can make a difference. Saying something is 'quite nice' is so bland that if applied to something that is hugely enjoyable it understates it so much as to be almost insulting. The emphasis may be inadequate but at least the word 'nice' makes it clear that something positive is being said.

Blandness – dealt with shortly – should certainly be avoided; it is unlikely to add power to what you describe. Choosing the wrong word is another matter. That might confuse, upset – or worse.

So before tackling anything more complicated, let's consider words. Simple single words, no problem there surely, you might say, or is there?

The following examples are designed to show the potential danger. Consider first a couple of simple everyday words: 'comic' and 'comical'. Mean much the same thing? No. Something 'comic' is intended to be funny, whereas something 'comical' is funny unintentionally. That's put banana skins in their place!

But more relevant to business writing are the following:

- 'Continuous' (unbroken or uninterrupted); 'continual' (repeated or recurring) – a project might be continuous (in process all the time), but work on it is more likely to be continual (unless you never sleep)
- Are you 'uninterested' in a proposal or 'disinterested' in it? The first implies you are apathetic and care not either way, the latter means you have nothing to gain from it
- Similarly, 'dissatisfied' and 'unsatisfied' should not be confused; disappointed or needing more of something respectively
- You might want to do something 'expeditiously' (quickly and efficiently), but saying it is 'expedient' might not be so well regarded since it means only that something is convenient (not always a good reason to do anything)
- 'Fortuitously' implies something happening accidentally; it does not mean 'fortunate'
- If you are a 'practical' person then you are effective, if something is 'practicable' it is merely possible or feasible to do, and 'pragmatic' is something meant to be effective (rather than proven to be so).

So, even one wrong word may do damage. More, especially in one sentence, quickly create nonsense: 'This pragmatic approach will ensure the practicable project will be continuous, it is fortuitous that I am uninterested in it and I am sure I will not be unsatisfied to see it start.'

Some words are regularly misused: 'objectives' and 'strategies', 'turnover' and 'profit', and more. It's clear that word selection is an area where some care is needed.

COACH'S TIP

Keep help at hand

Since care is clearly called for – literally word by word – some words may need to be checked. Always have a dictionary (and a thesaurus) close at hand, and check and pick carefully.

Of course, no inaccurate use of language will help you put a message over well even if it only annoys rather than confuses. As for example saying 'very unique' – unique means unlike anything else and cannot be qualified by 'very' in this way.

The company whose brochure I saw with the words 'very unique' occurring three times in one paragraph, does not in fact have a product that is 'better than' unique – even once. Writing '12 noon' when noon tells you everything you need to know; or talking about an ATM machine when the M stands for machine (an 'automated teller machine *machine*'?). Some care, maybe even some checking or study, may be useful.

COACHING SESSION 11

Analysis

Here you may like to turn to an example of your own writing (ideally a couple of pages in extent) and first check the language used for clarity, marking anything you feel, on reflection, is less clear than it might be and noting here any lessons you draw from the analysis that will avoid such mistakes in future writing.

CREATE READABILITY

Readability may be somewhat difficult to define, but we all know it when we experience it. Your writing must flow. One point must lead to another, the writing must strike the right tone, inject a little variety and, above all, there must be a logical and visible structure to carry the message along. As well as the shape, the technique of 'signposting' – briefly flagging what is to come – helps in a practical sense to get the reader to understand where something is going. It makes them read on, happy that the direction is sensible (this section starts just that way, listing the four points to come, of which 'readable' is the second). It is difficult to overuse signposting and it can be utilized at several levels within the text.

COACH'S TIP

An easy check

The easiest way to check that what you write flows well is to read it over – better still, do it out loud (or perhaps under your breath in an open-plan office!). You should then notice any awkwardness very easily.

COACHING SESSION 12

Making it flow

Return to your example (used in Coaching Session 11) and see if anything reads awkwardly. Mark changes and note the lessons below.

BE STRAIGHTFORWARD

Briefly stated, writing is best when put simply. Follow the principles of the well-known acronym KISS – 'Keep It Simple, Stupid'. Thus use:

- short words: Why 'elucidate' something when you can 'explain'? Why 'reimbursements' rather than 'expenses'? Similarly, although the verbs 'experiment' and 'test' do have slightly different meanings, in a general sense 'test' may be better; or you could use 'try'.
- short phrases: Do not say 'at this moment in time' when you mean 'now', or 'respectfully acknowledge' something, a suggestion perhaps, when you can simply say 'thank you for'.
- short sentences: A frequent characteristic of business reports is having too many overlong sentences. Short ones are good. However, they should be mixed in with longer ones, or reading becomes rather like the staccato action of a machine gun. Many reports contain sentences that are overlong, often because they mix two rather different points. Break these into two and the overall readability improves.
- short paragraphs: Depending on whether there are plenty of headings and bullet points it may be difficult to get this wrong, but keep an eye on it. Regular and appropriate breaks as the message builds make for easy reading.

Overall, this is one of the most important areas to bear in mind. It's a real asset if you can develop a kind of 'simple-ometer' that nudges you when you get too wordy. Incidentally, short can mean very short. A sentence can be just one word.

See!

And a paragraph can be just one short sentence.

Or it can be two sentences. Both short.

COACHING SESSION 13

Reducing (unnecessary) complexity

Return to your example (which you started using in Coaching Session 11) and read it over to see if anything seems unnecessarily complicated. Mark changes and note lessons below.

____

____

____

____

BE NATURAL

In the same way that some people are said to use a 'telephone voice', so some write in an unnatural fashion. Such a style may be termed old fashioned, bureaucratic or over-formal (most often the last-mentioned).

Such a style is made worse with attempts to create self-importance, or to make a topic seem weightier than it is. Just a few words can change the tone: saying 'the writer' can sound pompous, for instance, especially if there is no reason not to say 'I'.

COACH'S TIP

'Write the talk'

The lesson here is clear and provides a guide to good writing. Business documents *do* need some formality, but remember that they are a substitute for talking to people. They should resemble speech as closely as reasonably possible. Don't overdo this, either by becoming too chatty or by writing, say, 'won't' (which you might acceptably say), when 'will not' is genuinely more suitable.

However, if you compose what you write much as you would say it and then tighten it up, the end result is often better than when you set out to create something that is 'formal business writing'.

The four factors above have wide influence on writing style, but they do not act alone. Other points are important, and link to readers' expectations.

COACHING SESSION 14

Ensuring a natural tone

Return again to your example (which you started using in Coaching Session 11) and read it over this time to see if anything sounds unnatural. Mark changes and note lessons below.

____

____

____

____

READERS' DISLIKES

Writing needs to be based on what people say they want. This means writing that is: brief, succinct, relevant, precise, clear, and in 'our language'. Now, what do they *not* like?

Readers have expectations that what they must read will not be:

- **introspective**: It is appropriate in most business documents to use the word 'you' more than 'I' (or 'we', the company, the department, etc.). Thus saying: 'I will circulate more detailed information soon' might be better phrased as: 'You will receive more information (from me) soon'. More so, perhaps, if you add a phrase like: '... so that you can judge for yourselves.'

  This approach allows people to identify more easily with the situation described and is especially important if there is persuasion involved.
- **talking down**: 'As an expert, I can tell you that this must be avoided, you must never...' Bad start – it sounds condescending. You are only likely to carry people with you if you avoid this kind of thing.

  As a schools broadcast on radio put it: 'Never talk down to people, never be condescending. You *do* know what condescending *means* don't you?' Enough said!
- **biased**: At least where it intends not to be. A manager writing to staff setting out why she thinks something is a good idea, and then asking for the views of others, may elicit more agreement than is actually felt. If honest views are wanted, then it is better to simply set something out and ask for comment, without expressing a positive personal view in advance.
- **politically incorrect**: Nowadays, there is such sensitivity (oversensitivity?) about this issue that it should neither be ignored nor underestimated. It has its own heading in due course.

There is already a considerable amount to bear in mind here. The focus must be on the reader throughout. However, you must not forget your own position as the writer. There are elements here that must be incorporated into the way you write.

THE APPROPRIATE IMAGE

Every organization has an image. The only question is whether this just happens, for good or ill, or if it is seen as something to actively create, maintain and make positive. Similarly, every document you write says something about you. Whether you like it or not this is true. And it matters. The profile wittingly or unwittingly presented may influence whether people believe, trust or like you. It may influence how they feel about your expertise, or whether they can see themselves agreeing with you or doing business with you.

Your personal profile is not only an influence in your job, one that links to the objectives you have, it also potentially affects your career. Surely it is unavoidable that, given the profusion of paperwork in most organizations, what you write progressively typecasts you in the eyes of others – including your boss – as the sort of person who is going places, or not.

Image bears thinking about.

Certainly your prevailing style, and what a particular document says about you, is worth thinking about. If there is an inevitable subtext of this sort, you cannot afford to let it go by default; you need to consciously influence it.

Start by considering what you want people to think of you. Take a simple point. You want to be thought of as efficient. Then the style of the document surely says something about this. If it is good, contains everything the reader wants, and certainly if it covers everything it has promised, then a sense of efficiency surely follows. The same applies to many characteristics: being seen as knowledgeable, experienced, authoritative, and so on.

COACHING SESSION 15

Your profile

It is worth thinking through what personal characteristics you need or would like to project. Such as being thought of as being efficient, giving attention to detail, being approachable, well-organized, reliable, creative, interested in others, confident, experienced, expert – you may well be able to list more.

In respect of external communications, your corporate profile may include, for example, offering quality, value for money, sound (and honest) advice and having empathy. Again you may be able to think of more.

List those that are important here, and perhaps ascribe some priority to them.

1. Personal profile factors
2. Corporate profile factors

All such characteristics are worth considering to ascertain exactly how you achieve the effect you want. Such images are cumulative. They build up over time and can powerfully assist in the establishment and maintenance of relationships whether with a colleague, a customer or the boss (establishing that you are a good person to work with as well as being good at your work).

The point of thinking all this through is so that when you review something you have written you don't say to yourself: 'That's fine but I should add something that makes it clear that this comment [whatever it may be] is based on my expertise and experience.' Rather, you build in the emphasis you want as you go.

What you're not

Similarly, you might have in mind a list of characteristics that you actively want to avoid seeming to embrace. For example, you may not want to appear: dogmatic, patronizing, inflexible, old fashioned and more. While some characteristics can sometimes be emphasized, or even exaggerated, some cannot. Stubbornness is a good example.

Note: You could return to Coaching Session 15 adding the image factors to avoid.

Such images are not delivered in a single word. Certainly there is much more to appearing, say, honest than in your writing: 'Let me be completely honest' (which might actually just ring alarm bells!). Your intended profile will come, in part, from specifics such as choice of words, but also from the whole way in which you use language.

Of course inaccurate use of language will not help you get over your message, even if it only annoys rather than confuses (remember the 'very unique' example from earlier – repeated here because it is a particular twitch of mine and so regularly misused). Some care, maybe even some checking or study, may be useful, but let's consider some other areas of language use, first returning to political correctness mentioned earlier.

A WORD ABOUT... SEX

Political correctness may sometimes be taken to extremes but it cannot be ignored. (It is irresistible to use the word 'sex' as a heading, not least because books mentioning sex sell better than those that fail to do so!) More seriously, sexist language, together with inappropriate references to age, religion, ethnic origin and so on are not just unsuitable but can get you into serious trouble. Even minor transgressions can lead to people thinking of you in a different way.

Dwelling on obvious examples is, I am sure, not necessary; even an idiot would not write in a way that insults his or her readers; and that phrase is (intentionally) sailing close to the wind to make a point.

What needs to be done is to keep an eye on the way language is used and the way you use it. Clarity must always shine through – it is no good being politically careful but misunderstood. For example:

- The 'he/she' conundrum: Nowadays most people avoid an exclusive use of 'he' in case that seems to imply men only. Yet using 'she' throughout seems pretentiously contrived, and writing 'he or she' repeatedly can quickly become awkward or tedious, so a mixture of avoidance techniques is perhaps best.

  Gradually, the use of 'their' is changing so that writing: 'The boss called us into their office' is now more grammatically acceptable than previously.
- Time and terminology: Some words go through an evolution of usage. 'Chairman' is the sort of word that these trends largely outlawed, at least for a while; but now, although there is much use of 'Chair', many women seem happy to be a 'Chairman'. This sort of thing needs an eye keeping on it.
- Silly: Sometimes suggested changes seem to go too far. For example, I was pulled up the other day for talking about 'manning the office'. You should say, 'staffing' someone told me. But surely 'staffing the office' means recruiting people to work there, and 'manning it' means deciding who is on duty at different times to provide cover. Change here seems to me to risk a lack of clarity (and wouldn't doing so be just a little over-sensitive?).

This is an area where the sensitivities change over time and while there can be some silliness and over-sensitivity in evidence, the issue is important and deserves some careful consideration. Some mistakes are very much to be avoided, and you must write to fit in with particular and current practice.

MISTAKES TO AVOID

Numerous things may act to dilute the power of your writing. They may or may not be technically wrong, but they end up reducing your effectiveness and making your objectives less certain to be achieved. For example:

Blandness

As mentioned earlier, saying something is 'quite nice' is so bland that if applied to something that is hugely enjoyable it understates it so much as to be almost insulting. The emphasis may be inadequate but at least the word 'nice' makes it clear that something positive is being said.

So beware! This really is a common trap for the business writer, but it is worth emphasizing here. A bland feeling arises not so much because you wrote the wrong thing, but because you are writing on automatic pilot – without thought or at least *much* thought – and made no real conscious choice of wording.

What does it mean to say something is:

- *quite* good (or bad)?
- *rather* expensive?
- making *very* slow progress?

What exactly is:

- an *attractive* promotion? (As opposed to a profit-generating one, perhaps)
- a *slight* delay (for a moment or a month?)
- *some* improvement?
- a *practical* approach?

All these give only a vague impression. Ask yourself exactly what meaning you want to express, and then choose language that does just that. For example, is a *practical approach* one that is easy to do, quick to do – or both. Or something else altogether?

COACHING SESSION 16

Refining the right habits

Now you think about it, are there things that you do (and do regularly) that you would be better off not doing? They don't have to be outrageous errors, but if they dilute the effect you're aiming for they are best avoided. Have a think and record here any examples you want to bear in mind and avoid in future:

Recently, I had a sobering reminder of this kind of necessary care when I wrote something for a publisher with guidelines forbidding the use of the word 'key'. This is a word that tends to crop up pretty regularly in writing aimed at readers in the business world: 'key issues', 'key objectives' and more.

The instruction made me think. I checked another recent manuscript onscreen, clicking on Find and listing the 'key' (sic) word. I was amazed how many times it appeared in a manuscript of, I think, 40,000 words.

Alongside this I began to think of other options. I looked up the word 'crucial' in my thesaurus and went on from there. Soon I had listed many options – 'pivotal', 'critical', 'central', 'significant' and more – many of which, with precise and slightly different meanings, substituted for 'key' in a way that was more appropriate, and made the writing stronger and better.

I duly avoided the word key in the piece of writing in question and resolved to double-check its appropriateness every time I was tempted to use it elsewhere in future. You too may have favourite words you overuse and which could be replaced by words that are more accurately descriptive.

'Officespeak'

The word 'officespeak' may or may not appear in your dictionary, but it has come to describe another all-too-common component of some business writing, much of it passed on from one person to another without comment or change. It may confuse little, but adds little either.

Examples include phrases such as:

- 'Enclosed for your perusal' (even – 'Enclosed for your interest' – may be unsuitable. You may need to expand on why it should be of interest; or 'enclosed' alone may suffice)
- 'We respectfully acknowledge receipt of' (why not say 'Thank you for... '?)
- 'In the event that' ('If' is surely better)
- 'Very high speed operation' (try 'fast', or state just how fast)
- 'Conceptualized' (of thought).

You should avoid such trite approaches 'like the plague' (sic) – (see comments on clichés in due course) and work to change the habit of any 'pet' phrases you use all too easily, all too often and inappropriately. Also avoid sounding as if your main reference is not a dictionary but a jargon generator. Phrases such as, 'strategic re-engineered paradigm' or 'proactive, virtual integrated opportunity' just invite the reaction – 'What?' Or 'Idiot!'

Corporate 'officespeak'

Watch out for phrases that everyone around an organization has the habit of using. Some may be minor (why is so much referred to as 'proactive' when no one seems to be able to describe how it differs from 'active'?), or they may be more unsuitable. Resolve to avoid them.

Fashion in language

Changes to language occur all the time. New words and phrases enter the language almost daily, often from the US and also linked to the use of technology. It is worth watching for the life cycle of such words because if you are out of step then they may fail to do the job you want. I notice three stages:

1. When it is too early to use them. When they will either not be understood, or seem silly or even like a failed attempt at trendiness;
2. When they work well;
3. When their use begins to date and sound wrong or inadequate.

There's a danger in quoting examples, since they may date too, but let me try. When BBC Radio 4 talks about an 'upcoming' event, then for some people the expression is in its early stage of acceptability and does not sound right at all (certainly 'forthcoming' will suit me well for a while longer).

Conversely, what did we say before we said 'mission statement'? This is certainly a term in current usage. Most people in business appreciate its meaning and some have made good use of the thinking that goes into producing one.

Now consider a word or phrase that is past its best. To suggest a common one: 'user friendly'. When first used it was new, nicely descriptive and quickly began to be useful. Now, with no single gadget on the entire planet not so described by its makers, it has become weak to say the least.

Making people twitch

There are some grammar errors that are actually well known to most people, yet they still slip through, and there is yet another category of error that annoys many people when they are on the receiving end.

A simple, but important example, mentioned earlier, is the word 'unique', which is so often used with a qualifying adjective. Further errors of this type include the likes of:

- 'Different to' (it should be 'different from')
- 'Less' (which relates to a quantity). When a specific number is involved 'fewer' is the correct usage
- 'Can' being confused with 'may' ('possible' and 'permissible' meanings respectively).

COACHING SESSION 17

Removing the twitches

Think of similar 'twitch-making' examples that annoy you and attempt to avoid them too.

Another area for care is with unnecessary apostrophe's (sic), which are becoming a modern plague (even Lynne Truss's wonderful book *Eats, Shoots & Leaves* has not managed to reverse the trend). Incorrect apostrophes have become known as the greengrocer's apostrophe because of the prevalence of such signs on stalls declaring 'lovely ripe apple's'.

Clichés

Clichés present a somewhat difficult consideration. Any overused phrase can become categorized as a cliché. Yet a phrase like 'putting the cart before the horse' is not only well known, but establishes an instant and precise vision - and can therefore be useful.

In a sense, people like to conjure up a familiar image and so such phrases should not always be avoided, and business documents may not be the place for creative alternatives like 'spread the jam before the butter'.

Use 'Find'

If there is any sort of mistake that you want to avoid, it may be useful to check your habits. You can go to an electronic file and enter a phrase in Find (say, 'very unique' or whatever) and see how often it appears. Doing this is sometimes sobering – and useful.

RULES TO FOLLOW

This book does not attempt to provide a comprehensive guide to correct English usage, though some points are mentioned as a reminder and as a spur to establishing the right habits and you may feel these and others need more study.

Keep (more) help to hand

You may find a grammar guide a useful desk-side companion. Something accessible like *Good Word Guide* (Bloomsbury) or Bill Bryson's *Troublesome Words* (Penguin); there is a profusion of books like this from which to choose.

Grammar, **syntax** and **punctuation** all need care – they matter – so too does spelling, but computer spellcheckers can make up for any inadequacies in that area these days; though you still need to 'cheque (sic)' carefully since there are plenty of possibilities for error.

But some of the rules are made to be broken and some of the old rules are no longer regarded as relevant, certainly not for business writing.

Double check

Use a computer spellchecker by all means but be aware of the things it cannot help with – for example, proper names (spell a client's name wrongly and you may upset a whole relationship).

Some things certainly jar. Consider just a few examples:

- Poor punctuation: Too little is exhausting to read, especially coupled with long sentences. Too much can seem contrived and awkward. Certain rules do matter here, but the simplest guide is probably to listen to your breathing.

  We learn to punctuate speech long before we write anything, so in writing the rudimentary idea is to be conscious of the natural pauses. The length of pause and the nature of what is being said dictate the likely course of action. In some ways, better too much than not enough.
- Tautology: This is unnecessary repetition of which the classic example is people who say 'I, myself personally' and is to be avoided. Do not 'export overseas', simply 'export', do not indulge in 'forward planning', simply 'plan'.
- Oxymorons: These are word combinations that are contradictory and which may sound silly or inappropriate – 'distinctly foggy' – 'definite maybe' – or be current good ways of expressing something – 'deafening silence'. Some sentences can cause similar problems of contradiction – 'I never make predictions; and I never will'.

Other things that are still regarded as rules by purists work well in business writing and are common in everyday use. For example, there's the traditional rule stating that you should never begin a sentence with the words 'and' or 'but'. But you can. And it helps to produce tighter writing and avoids overlong sentences. However, it also makes another point: do not overuse this sort of thing.

A similar rule is that sentences cannot end in a preposition. Yet 'He is a person worth talking to' really is easier on the ear than: 'Yet he is a person with whom it is worth talking.'

Memorably, Winston Churchill is said to have responded to criticism with the famous line: 'This is the type of arrant pedantry up with which I will not put.'

Other rules may be broken only occasionally. Many of us have been brought up never to split infinitives! There are exceptions however: would the most famously quoted one in the world – *Star Trek*'s 'to boldly go where no man has gone before' – really be better as 'to go boldly…'? I do not think so.

LANGUAGE THAT WORKS FOR YOU

The way language is used makes a difference to exactly how a message is received. The importance of using the right word has already been touched on, but the kind of difference we are talking about can be well demonstrated by changing no more than one word.

For example, consider the first sentence after the last heading: 'The way language is used makes a difference to exactly how a message is received.' Add one word '… makes a *big* difference to…'

Now, let's continue and see what changing that word 'big' makes: it is surely a little different to say: …'makes a *great* difference'…. and there are many options, all with varying meaning: 'real', 'powerful', 'considerable', 'vast', 'special', 'large', 'important'. You can doubtless think of more. In context of what I am saying here, 'powerful' is a good word. It is not just a question of how you use language, but what you achieve by your use of it.

Using appropriate description

Rather than dwell on mistakes, let's think positively. English is on your side. It is perfectly possible to create powerful descriptions; often this can be done in remarkably few words. Consider a general example: an account (from Peter Mayle's book *A Year in Provence*) describes a visitor to the house (the book is about renovating a house in rural France). He arrives with an attractive young lady (who is described in some detail) and he shows her up the steps ahead of him. The only thing that is said about him is that he was 'A man who could give lessons in leering.' Is there anything else you need to know?

Even something as routine as a classified advertisement can make this point, for example: 'For sale: baby's cot – unused'. Have you ever read an ad that conjures up so much heartache?

Business writing is often almost devoid of adjectives. Yet surely one of the first purposes of language is to be descriptive. Most writing necessitates the need to paint a picture to some degree at least. Contrast two phrases:

- 'Smooth as silk'
- 'Sort of shiny'.

The first (used as a slogan by Thai Airways) conjures up a clear and precise picture; or certainly does for anyone who has seen and touched silk. The second might mean almost anything; dead wet fish are sort of shiny, but they are hardly to be compared with the touch of silk.

Further, an even more descriptive phrase may be required: I once heard the following phrase on the radio: 'slippery as a freshly buttered ice-rink'. Could anyone think this meant other than really, really slippery?

The expectation of complexity (and cognitive cost) was mentioned earlier, and to some extent it does not matter whether something is short or long; if it makes things effortlessly clear, it is appreciated. And if it is both descriptive and makes something easier to understand then readers are doubly appreciative.

Clear description may need working at, but the effort is worthwhile. Trainers often ask meeting venue staff to set up for a seminar by arranging the participants 'in a U-shape'. You can put people in a U around a boardroom-style table. But more often trainers mean a U in the sense of an open U, one that gives the trainer the ability to stand within the U to work and communicate with delegates. There are, in fact, two different layouts described here, both of which demand precise description.

COACHING SESSION 18

Making description powerful

Recall or find some examples of descriptions you use regularly, for instance about your organization, products or services. List them and see if they strike you as sufficiently clear and powerful; if not, think of and list options.

Description is important, but sometimes we want more than that. We want writing to be memorable: descriptive yet unusual or descriptive and unexpected.

Let's return to the venue theme above. If a conference executive describes a U shape as one that: 'puts everyone in the front row' they are being descriptive and memorable because it is also an unusual way of expressing it (and just how a trainer sees it). Such viewpoints work well and are thus worth searching for.

Here is an example of the second route to being memorable. I will use a description I once put in a report. In summarizing a Perception Survey I had conducted (researching the views customers and contacts had of a trade association), I wanted to describe how the majority of people reported back. They liked them, were well disposed towards using them, but also found them a little bureaucratic, slow and less efficient and innovative than they would ideally like. I wrote that they were seen as 'being like a comfortable, but threadbare old sofa, when people wanted them to be like a modern, leather executive chair'. This is clearly descriptive, but it gained not just from being unusual, but by being atypical in business writing.

It was memorable because it rang bells and at subsequent meetings was used by the organization's own people to describe the changes that the report had highlighted as necessary.

There are occasions where this kind of approach works well, not least in ensuring something about the writer is expressed along the way. Some phrases or passages may draw strength because the reader would never feel it was quite appropriate to put it like that themselves, yet find they like reading it.

Another aspect you may want, on occasion, to put into your writing is **emotion**. If you want to seem enthusiastic, interested, surprised – whatever – this must show. A dead, expressionless style '... the results were not quite as expected, they showed that...' is not the same as one that characterizes what is said with emotion '...you will be surprised by the results, which showed that...' Both may be appropriate on occasion, but the latter is sometimes avoided when it could add to the sense and feeling; and there might be occasion to strengthen that – 'the results will amaze'.

COACH'S TIP

Just do it

Consider this. How often when you are searching for the right phrase do you reject something as either not sufficiently formal or not conventional? Be honest. Many people hover on the brink of putting down something that will be memorable or that will add power, and then they play safe and opt for something else. The alternative selected may be adequate, but may fail to impress; and may well then represent a lost opportunity. Have the courage of your convictions.

YOUR PERSONAL STYLE

Finally, most people have or develop a way of writing that includes words and phrases they simply like. Why not indeed? For example, although the rule books now say they are simply alternatives, some people, myself included, think that to say: 'First,... secondly... and thirdly...' has much more elegance than beginning: 'Firstly...' The reason why matters less than achieving an effect you feel is right. Besides, my example and preference is the traditional way!

Now it would be a dull old world if we all did everything the same way and writing is no exception. There is no harm in using some words or phrases for no better reason than you like them. It is likely to add variety to your writing, and make it seem distinctively different from that of other people, which may itself be useful.

Certainly you should always be happy that what you write sounds right. So, to quote the writer Keith Waterhouse: 'If, after all this advice, a sentence still reads awkwardly, then what you have there is an awkward sentence. Demolish it and start again.'

ONLINE RESOURCE

Checking (and checking)

It's so important to get every detail right, and to give you another way of resolving to check everything carefully, you might find the following amusing. Though I take a light-hearted approach, it does reinforce the many points made, and show just how crucial it is to be wary when writing.

www.TYCoachbooks.com/BusinessWriting

COACH'S TIP

Another reference

The quote above is from a book by Keith Waterhouse titled *English our English*. It is now out of print, though it is still possible to find copies online. It is the best overall guide to writing and language I know, and is certainly one of only a few that is fun to read.

NEXT STEPS

This chapter has focused on language and the ways in which it can best be used. Two things predominate here:

- Avoiding errors of any kind that dilute the impact sought
- Maximizing the clarity and effectiveness of your writing by attention to detail in the way you write.

In the next chapter the focus remains on language, but focuses on getting the style of writing correct to fit the task and the particular communication method involved.

This section is designed to give you a moment to take stock. You may decide to read on, return to earlier coaching sessions or make some notes of progress to date and factors likely to be important to you in the future. Some notes in response to the questions here may prove useful as you proceed.

Having read this chapter do you feel better able to judge the effectiveness of your writing? And, if so, what specific lessons do you draw about your prevailing practice? Note them here.

Note what particular practices (perhaps habits) you want to avoid?

Note what particular practices you can usefully aim to add or adapt and make work harder?

Note which changes would make for the greatest improvement in your writing?

5

HOW TO WRITE PERSUASIVELY

OUTCOMES FROM THIS CHAPTER

- In this chapter we move on to a very particular aspect of language and set out how to make a persuasive case using some basic techniques. You can make a convincing case and secure agreement using the psychology of persuasive language.

AN ADDED DIMENSION

A surprising number of business messages are designed to persuade. They may be directed internally or externally and include everything from an email to letters, reports and proposals.

We'll go beyond the difficulties of making communication work well and look at the elements contained in a message that aims to persuade, and see how writing can influence the way in which people make decisions.

People are often suspicious of someone 'with something to sell'. Persuasion is synonymous with selling and selling does not, let's be honest, have a very good image.

Consider your own reaction to someone trying to sell you double glazing or insurance, particularly when it is done inexpertly or inappropriately. Every persuasive message pushes the same reaction buttons as those generated by the worst kind of selling.

THE BASIC APPROACH

Specifically, people who receive your persuasive messages may feel:

- insecure
- threatened
- at risk
- impatient
- worried

- ignorant
- sceptical
- suspicious
- fearful.

Indeed, they may feel several at one time. For example, an internal document about a new policy or way of doing something may make an employee feel sceptical (thinking it won't work, perhaps based on prior experience) and insecure, at risk and worried (asking will I cope with this?). Your approach must be to reduce and conquer these kinds of feeling.

How do you do this?

Essentially, you start by adopting the right attitude to the process. Before you write anything you need to approach it in the right way. Persuasion must not be regarded as a process of 'doing something to people'. Rather it should be seen as working with people. After all, any viable communication involves more than one person.

When presented with a possible course of action most people want to make up their *own* minds about it, indeed they will instinctively weigh up the case presented to them and make a considered decision.

The amount of conscious weighing up undertaken will depend on how people judge the importance of the decision. If you ask someone in the office – 'can you spare time for a drink at lunchtime so that we can discuss the next scheduled departmental meeting?' – they may hardly need to think about it at all. It will only last a few minutes, they have to have a bite to eat anyway, and they already know about the meeting and want to be involved. Ask or write to them about something more substantial and the weighing-up process will involve more; maybe much more.

FOCUS ON THE RECIPIENT

Persuasion is perhaps best defined as being a process of helping people weigh up something and so make a decision about it. When you aim to persuade you are helping people decide. It follows, therefore, that you need to understand how they actually go about this process.

Paraphrasing psychologists who have studied it, this thinking process can be described in simple terms thus: People...

- consider the factors that make up a case;
- seek to categorize these as advantages or disadvantages;
- weigh up the complete case, allowing for all the pluses and minuses;
- select a course of action (which may be simply agreeing or not, or involve the choice of one action being taken rather than another) that reflects the overall picture.

Let us be clear. What is going on here is not a search for perfection. Most conclusions we come to have some inevitable downsides. (This may be the most useful book you've ever read, but reading it does take some time that could be used for something else. This disappearing time might well be seen as a downside.)

A useful analogy

The analogy of a set of weighing scales is worth keeping in mind. It can act as a practical tool, helping you picture what is going on in someone's mind during a persuasive approach. Beyond that, it helps structure the process if you also have a clear idea of the sequence of thinking involved in this weighing-up process.

Continuing the weighing scales analogy, it is worth bearing in mind that the pluses and minuses on either side can be of any weight: one additional small point can gain or lose an entire agreement.

The thinking process

One way of looking at what is going on is to think of people moving through several stages of thinking, as if they were saying to themselves:

- **I matter most.** Whatever you want me to do, I expect you to worry about how I feel about it, respect me and consider my needs
- **What are the merits and implications of the case you make?** Tell me what you suggest and why it makes sense (the pluses) and whether it has any snags (the minuses) so that I can weigh it up – bearing in mind that few, if any, propositions are a perfect fit
- **How will it work?** Here, people want to assess the details of the areas associated with the proposal.

  For example, you might want to persuade a colleague to take on or become involved with a project. The idea of the project might appeal, but if it ends up with the person having to prepare a lengthy written report, he might see that as a chore (a minus) and if the case is finely balanced he might reject it on those grounds
- **What do I do?** In other words, what action – exactly – is now necessary? This too forms part of the balance. If during a quick flick through of this book you saw something that persuaded you that it might help you, you may have impulsively bought it. In doing so you recognized (and accepted) that you would have to read the book and that it would take a little time.

  The action – reading – is inherent in the proposition and if you were not prepared to take it on this might have changed your decision.

Once this thinking is complete people will feel they have sufficient evidence on which to base a decision. They have the balance in mind, and they can compare it with that of any other options (remember that some choices are close run and turn on a single issue). Then they can decide and feel they have made a sensible decision, and done so on a considered basis.

This thinking process is largely universal. It may happen very quickly and might be almost instantaneous – the snap judgement. Or it may take longer, maybe days or weeks (or longer!) rather than minutes or hours. But it is always in evidence. There is always merit in setting out your case in a way than sits comfortably alongside the way in which it will be considered. Hence the definition mentioned that describes persuasion as helping the decision-making process.

This thinking process should not be difficult to identify with; it is simply what happens when you consider buying something or have a decision to consider.

COACHING SESSION 19

How you decide

If you need convincing of the truth of this then it is worth imagining how you make such decisions. Think of an example, something that demands some time to consider, especially in terms of differentiating between one thing and another. For example, if you were to purchase a new television, there would be numerous things to assess, both technical (should it be 'smart' and linked to the Internet, what size suits your living room, price, possible delivery dates and set up, and more).

Picking your own example and noting how much there is to consider, both tangible and intangible points, will show you the extent of the decision-making process and why the weighing scales analogy makes sense.

Essentially, all that is necessary when attempting to persuade is to keep this thinking process ongoing and address the individual points in turn. Thus you need to:

- **start by demonstrating a focus on the other person** – it also helps to create some rapport and make clear how you aim to put things over
- **present a balanced case** – you need to stress the positive, of course, but not to pretend there may be no snags, especially if they are manifest. So present a clear case, give it sufficient explanation and weight and recognize the balancing decision the recipient will undertake
- **add in working details** – mention how things will work, include ancillary details especially those that will matter to others.

In this way, when you set out a case the structure and logic of it should sensibly follow this pattern. Otherwise the danger is that you will be trying to do one thing while the person you are communicating with is doing something else.

Make no mistake: people will do what they want and especially so when they are reading something and you are not there to try to draw them back to your viewpoint.

PERSUASION'S MAGIC FORMULA

The word 'persuasion' is defined in the dictionary broadly thus: 'to cause (a person) to believe or do something by reasoning with them'. Fine, but the question is *how* to do this. To be persuasive a case must be understandable, attractive and credible.

COACHING SESSION 20

Select an example

Think of an example of a message you must put over that must be persuasive; bear this in mind and we will return to it specifically in due course with a task for you to work on.

Now, consider the three factors just mentioned in turn:

CREATE UNDERSTANDING

A good deal has already been said about the need for clear communication. The point here is more than simply avoiding misunderstandings. People like clarity of explanation and ease of understanding. Making readers spend five minutes reading endless text that goes round the houses, only to have the light dawn at the last moment in a way that gets the person thinking 'why didn't you say that to begin with?' hardly builds your credibility.

When people expect something to be difficult to understand and it turns out to be easy, it's understandable that they like it. A powerful description, especially one that puts things in terms the other person can identify with, can strengthen a case disproportionately. Care is sensible here. Avoid inappropriate use of jargon: it is only useful shorthand when both parties have the same level of understanding of what is involved, perhaps in a specialist area. You only have to think about the vast range of terms linked to the world of information technology to observe the problem. So, always:

- think about explanations and descriptions, try them out and be sure they work
- aim to make what you write immediately and easily understood
- be thorough and precise, giving people enough detail to make your point and emphasizing the most relevant elements
- match with the other person the level of technicality you use (and avoid or explain jargon if it might confuse).

Creating easy understanding is certainly an area where you can score some points.

COACH'S TIP

Signposting what is to come

Think about the structure and sequence of what you write and how it breaks down into subsections. Present a logical and organized case and signal what you aim to do in advance – 'it may be easiest if I present this in stages. Let me refer to the timing first, then the costs, and then how we need to organize implementation.' If such a start gets people nodding – 'that seems sensible' – then you will carry them with you to the next pages. Use as many layers of this as is necessary to keep things clear. For example, adding – 'timing implies when we will do things and how long it will take, so duration is taken first, then it is easier to see when things can be fitted in.'

Already what you achieve in this respect can begin to put some convincing pluses on the positive side of your balance.

COACHING SESSION 21

Creating understanding (example)

Take the case you identified earlier that needed to be made more persuasive. Note here your thoughts about what will help make the case clear. What will need care, what approach, indeed words, will be best?

Note the gist of your thinking here (we will return to continue work on this example in due course).

MAKE THE CASE ATTRACTIVE

This part of the argument has to set out the core pluses of the case, painting a picture of why agreement should follow. You get your own way when people see what something does for, or means to, them. How this is done is largely a question of giving the argument a focus on what, in sales jargon, are called 'benefits', rather than 'features'. So:

- **a benefit** is what something does for or means to someone.
- **features** are simply factual points about it.

The spellchecker on a computer is a feature. Being able to produce an accurate manuscript quickly and easily, the time and effort saved and the avoidance of material being returned for correction (by a boss or customer) are all benefits. They are things the feature – the spellchecker – allows to happen for me. Features act to produce benefits.

The sequence here is important. Just tell people everything about a suggestion in terms of its features and their response may well be to say (or think), 'So what?' Start by focusing their thinking, show them that what you are suggesting fits that scenario and then the feature may reinforce the argument.

Benefits in action

How you use this approach makes a difference. For instance, you could say something will 'save you money', or that it will 'save money and recoup its costs in a month', or it will 'halve what you spend'. If the description matches the circumstances of the reader, and if it specifically rings bells because of how it is described, then this will work best.

Consider a product example. A company sells commercial cooking equipment to restaurants and cafes. One product is flat grills. One feature is the size: there are various models and one has a cooking surface of 800 square centimetres. What is the benefit? It will cook a dozen eggs or six steaks simultaneously.

Now most people find it difficult to conjure up the idea of 800 square centimetres, but everyone who runs a restaurant will be able to imagine the eggs and steaks with no problem at all. Link the way this is described to their situation further – imagine the rush you get at breakfast time – and it makes a powerful point.

If you always keep in mind what something does for or means to other people you will be able to write text that will put over a more powerful case. The phrase 'benefit-led' is used in selling and that is a good way of thinking about it. Benefits come first, features explain how that is possible and, if necessary, you can add additional credibility (of which more anon).

For example: This book is called *The Business Writing Coach* (feature). 'It will help you get a message across effectively and, when necessary, to obtain agreement from others' (benefit), which will save arguments and get more done (further benefit). 'The methods it describes are tried and tested and their presentation in training courses have received positive feedback' (evidence; to which might be added a positive comment from a named delegate or training organization). The idea of teasing out the way you put things by saying 'which means that...' and seeing where that takes you is a good one. Start with a feature and at the end of the line you will assuredly have a benefit, maybe more than one.

Prior to writing you can do worse than list all the things that people might obtain from your ideas. Some may be classic, others may be more individual to whatever you are writing about.

What's in it for me?

As a result of agreeing with you people might be able to:

- make more money
- save money
- save time, effort or hassle
- be more secure
- sort out problems
- be able to exploit opportunities
- motivate others (e.g. staff)
- impress people (e.g. customers).

Let's take the example of two people involved in a presentation, one wanting to get together to prepare. Say – 'a rehearsal will only take an hour' – (the duration is a feature) and it may leave someone cold or get them saying – 'How long?' in horror at what they see as a long time. Get them agreeing that the presentation must go well – 'Yes, it must.' That there is a great deal to gain from it – 'Right' – and that there is a possibility of two presenters falling over each other's feet unless there is a rehearsal – 'Could be.' Then the 'ability of the rehearsal to increase the chances of success' – (which is what it will do and thus a benefit) makes much better sense.

The task is therefore to make a clear case to people, to emphasize aspects of the case that reflect their priorities – and have a positive effect on the other person and to make sure there are sufficient, and sufficiently powerful, pluses to add up to an agreeable proposition.

COACH'S TIP

Appropriate weight

There is interesting research showing that just the right amount of weight to a case helps to persuade. Something in the bracket 4 to 7 main benefits seems to work best (enough to [illegible] many as to make the [illegible] confused or boring). This is catalogued in the book *Killer Presentations*, Nick Oulton (How to Books).

COACHING SESSION 22

Making the case attractive (example)

Now revisit the plan you made earlier to make persuasive. Here just note any thoughts about what will help make the case attractive. What will need care, what approach, indeed words, will be best?

Note the gist of your thinking here to continue to build up the picture.

ADD CREDIBILITY

Because of the inherent suspicion that tends to exist when selling or persuasion are in evidence, people's reaction to your saying that something is a good course of action to adopt may simply be to say – 'you would say that wouldn't you!' Your say so is not enough. Never rely on that alone, but seek and build in evidence.

This could be sheer numbers (thousands of customers can't be wrong), or tests, guarantees or standards met or complied with. It must be clear that the case is really sound. The salesperson selling a car who says – 'the Automobile Association test results show it does 55 miles per gallon' – is putting a reliable source ahead of the figure they want to quote, and boosting the weight it adds to their argument. This makes it so much more likely to be believed than simply saying, 'it will do 55 miles to the gallon'.

Such credibility can be added in many ways, for example:

- Quoting past experience: 'The project approach is very like... and that worked well.'
- Involving the support of others (a person or organization): 'The Training Manager reckons a rehearsal of the presentation would be useful.' (useful when the other party respects the person being referred to)
- Quoting measurement of results: '50 per cent of this kind of presentation ends without securing agreement; let's make sure this is one of the successful ones.'
- Mentioning any guarantees, tests or standards that are met
- Invoking weight of argument that reinforces the case: 'Several departments work this way already/hundreds of people use it.'

Before exposing any case to others, it is worth thinking both about the need for proof and how strong that need might be, and thus what evidence can be used in support of your argument.

COACH'S TIP

Several people

A final point here: remember that a person's perspective on something may not be solely their own. Someone might behave with their employer or department, their boss, their family, or their staff in mind. Equally, they may react positively for reasons of common good, because their helping you will help make the department you both work for more efficient perhaps, or very personally, they want to be seen to be involved in something or you promise them a drink in the pub. This may mean you need to direct, in part, your aim at these other people.

COACHING SESSION 23

Adding credibility

Now you can complete the case you picked earlier to make it persuasive. Here just note any thoughts about what will help make the case credible. What will need care, what approach, indeed words, will be best?

Note the gist of your thinking here to complete the picture.

USING LANGUAGE *PERSUASIVELY*

People seldom read a letter, say, immediately, and rarely in the same sequence in which it was written. First, their eyes flick from the sender's address to the ending, then to the greeting and perhaps the first sentence. They fix on headings, they skim to the end – and then, if the sender has written well, go back to the first sentence for a more careful reading of the whole letter from the beginning. A letter is just an example: the same principle applies to other documents, even a short email.

You must always present a message people will really consider, and nowhere is this more true than when you aim to persuade. This is something worth bearing in mind as you write and reinforces the point made earlier about earning a reading. In fact for some writing it may be worth calling a powerful image to mind.

I always think of the training film *The Proposal* (Video Arts), which I sometimes use on courses. It starts with a sales person writing a proposal and imagining its receipt. We see the buyer (actor John Cleese) expressing overpowering delight at its arrival. He clears his desk, cancels meetings, tells his secretary he must not be disturbed and settles down to read. Then the voice-over says, 'But it's not like that is it?' The scene changes, and this time when the document arrives we see a surly John Cleese sitting miserably at his desk dropping Alka-Seltzers into a glass and wincing at the noise they make.

Maybe that is who we should imagine writing for!

A PERSUASIVE *STRUCTURE*

When communicating face to face, you can adapt your approach to the individual you are with as the conversation proceeds. This is not possible with the written word and a formula to structure the approach is useful.

The classic sales acronym AIDA stands for:

A Attention: first get them reading and wanting to know more

I Interest: then develop their interest and make them want to read on to complete the picture

D Desire: aim to turn interest into an actual acceptance or desire for something

A Action: conclude by asking clearly for the action you want to be taken.

This provides a simple structure and works well in providing a plan to help compose persuasive messages and represents accurately the job to be done in prompting a response. Each stage is worth elaboration as follows:

Attention – the opening

Unsurprisingly perhaps, an important part of any letter is the start. It may well determine whether the rest of the letter is read. The opening may be quite short, a heading (there should always be a heading), a couple of sentences, two paragraphs, but it is disproportionately important. A good start will help as you write the letter, as well as making it more likely the recipient will read it. Omit or keep references short and make subject headings to the point - the reader's point.

Do not use 'Re' (meaning 'regarding'). It is old fashioned and was once used in front of a heading to show that it was a heading before it was easy to emphasize it with, say, bold type. Make sure the start of the letter commands attention, gains interest and leads easily into the main text. For example:

- Ask a 'Yes' question
- Explain why you are writing to that reader particularly
- Explain why the reader should read the letter
- Flatter the reader (carefully)
- Explain what might be lost if the reader ignores the message
- Give the reader some 'mind-bending' news (if you have any).

Interest/desire – the body of the letter

The body of the letter runs straight on from the opening. It must consider the reader's needs, problems or situation from their point of view. It must interest them. It must get them nodding in agreement: 'Yes, I wish you could help me on that' or 'that sounds interesting'.

In drafting your message you must respond to their thinking and write what you intend for the readers and then describe the benefits you can offer (not features, remember), and in particular the benefits that will help them solve their problems or satisfy their needs.

Anticipating the reader's possible objectives to your proposition is important in order to allow you to accurately select your strongest benefits and most convincing answers. If there is a need to counter objections, then you may need to make your letter longer and give proof; for example, comment from a third party that the benefits are genuine. However, remember to keep letters as short as possible, though still as long as necessary. If that takes two, three or more pages, so be it.

It is easy to find yourself quoting full chapter and verse down to the last detail. If you were writing a lecture on the subject, you would probably need all that information. More usually you have to select just the key benefits that will be of particular value to the reader and that support any accompanying literature.

The central text must:

- keep the reader's immediate interest
- develop that interest with the best benefit
- win the reader over with a second benefit and then further benefits, sufficient to produce a powerful case.

The end – securing agreement and prompting action

The next job is to ensure action from the reader by a firm close (as sales jargon calls it). This may need to summarize, but beyond that the most important thing to do is to state clearly the action or agreement you want.

So next consider the final words used in persuasive writing and their relationship to your intention to prompt action. In closing it may be useful to make a (short) summary of the benefits of the proposition.

Having decided on the action you want the reader to take, you must make it absolutely clear to them what it is.

I was once involved in a project with a professional association that was changing its subscription arrangement so that payment had to be made by direct debit. The instructions seemed crystal clear, but people managed to misinterpret them somehow and the association's secretary's telephone rang regularly with members on the line with queries.

If people can misinterpret something, they will and you must... Enough. Suffice to say that any reference to action must be clear, and that means spelling it out *very carefully*.

Reply cards sent with (good) direct mail provide a lesson for us. They are as well produced and important looking as the rest of the mail shot. They often reinforce or repeat their message more than once, for example, the telephone number to be called is printed in bold or may well be highlighted in, say, colour. Similarly, the instructions, carefully analysed, smack of belt and braces; it is perfectly sensible and something that suggests a valuable lesson.

It is necessary to nudge the reader into action with a decisive close. Do not use phrases like these:

- 'We look forward to hearing...'
- 'I trust you have given...'
- '...favour of your instructions'
- 'Your support will be appreciated'
- 'I hope I can be of further assistance'.

By all means offer further assistance or information, but don't suggest incompleteness or inadequacy, with phrases such as, 'if you have any queries...' In a letter many such phrases are only really added as padding between the last point and 'Yours sincerely'. They are clichéd and add nothing except an old-fashioned feel or, worse, a feeling of uncertainty and circumspection. Instead, use real closing phrases.

The alternative close:

Ask the reader:

- to telephone or write
- to telephone or use the reply-paid envelope
- to ask for a meeting or more information.

Immediate gain:

A phrase like 'Return the card today and your profitability could be improved' offers something extra, or seemingly extra, if action is taken now rather than later. The converse of this is called a **fear close**, for example, phrasing something to say 'Unless you respond now something good will be missed'.

'Best' solution:

A phrase that summarizes key issues mentioned earlier: 'You want a system that can cope with occasional off-peak demands, that is easy to operate by semi-skilled staff and is presented in a form that will encourage line managers to use it. The best fit with all these requirements is our system "X".' Return the card indicating the best time to install it... that then links to a closing statement

Direct request:

Just a straight request, or even, on occasion, an instruction:

- 'Post the card back today'
- 'Telephone me without delay'.

If a message is impersonal it can put people off taking action, so if something like a letter is going to a mailing list of people, make sure it is addressed appropriately.

Consider too the person who should have their name at the bottom of the letter. Replies will tend to come back to them - and so will queries. So for a sales letter, for example, should it be the sales office, one director or another and how well are they able to cope with needing to respond?

Make sure the signatory's name is typed as well, since signatures tend to be awkward to read, and that the position they hold in the firm is included. People like to know with whom they are dealing; indeed they dislike it if they do not.

COACHING SESSION 24

Overall structure

Now you can continue to plan how you can make persuasive the case you picked earlier. Here, note any thoughts about what will help make the overall case flow logically and do a good job. What will need care, what approach, indeed words, will be best?

Note the gist of your thinking here (If you did not do so before, taking a new – real – example to assist you actually write something necessary may be worthwhile).

PS:

Consider the power of the postscript in persuasive messages. Past practice may tell you they are for things inadvertently left out, but direct mailers will tell you they really do get read. Ensure the wording of the postscript makes clear it is not about something accidentally omitted, but is there to provide emphasis. Use them in general to reinforce an important point or to add a final benefit – their use can add strength to many messages.

AN APPROPRIATE TONE

Returning to the language you use: it must be clear, appropriate and have sufficient impact to persuade. The following points add to those made in the last chapter, starting with a checklist that recaps and sets out some basic rules for persuasive copy.

- Be clear: Make sure that the message is straightforward and uncluttered by 'padding'. Use short words and phrases. Avoid jargon
- Be natural: Do not project yourself differently just because it is in writing
- Be positive: In tone and emphasis (be helpful)
- Be courteous: Always (ditto politically correct)
- Be efficient: Project the right image
- Be personal: Use 'I' – say what *you* will do, though focus on the reader throughout
- Be appreciative: 'Thank you' is a good phrase.

The next checklist, set out below, examines certain specific aspects of the language usefully used in persuasive communications. All these examples are very much the kind of phrases that do *not* lend themselves to persuasion; while one or two such words or phrases may do no great harm, if this kind of style predominates then a wholly wrong one is set. So:

Avoid trite openings, such as:

- 'We respectfully suggest...'
- 'We have pleasure in attaching...'
- 'Referring to the attached...'
- 'This letter is for the purposes of requesting...'

Avoid pomposity, such as:

- 'We beg to advise...'
- 'The position with regard to...'
- 'It will be appreciated that...'
- 'The undersigned/the writer...'
- 'May we take this opportunity of...'
- 'Allow me to say in this instance...'
- 'Having regard to the fact that...'
- 'We should point out that...'
- 'We are not in a position to...'
- 'The opportunity is taken to mention...'

Avoid clichéd endings, such as:

- 'Thanking you in advance...'
- 'Assuring you of our best attention at all times, we remain...'
- 'Trusting we may be favoured with...'
- 'Awaiting a favourable reply...'
- 'Please do not hesitate to...'

Your text must be positive. It should say: 'this is the case, this is what will be done' and will rarely say things like 'I think', 'probably', 'maybe' or 'perhaps'.

COACH'S TIP

From the world of direct mail

Experienced direct mailers talk about 'magic' words, by which they mean words that inject a tone that should always be present and that add to the intended persuasiveness. Examples include:

free	today	timely
guarantee(d)	win	respected
new	easy	reliable
announcing	save	opportunity
you	at once	low cost
now	unique	fresh
introducing	proven	gain

Note: My Teach Yourself book *Direct Marketing In A Week* may be a useful reference if you want to explore more of the chapter and verse of direct mail.

You must not overuse such words or your message will become blatantly over the top, but do not neglect them either.

FURTHER USEFUL TECHNIQUES

You must keep searching for ways of making your chosen text perform better. Again, the following is designed not only to suggest and highlight some examples, but also to show the approach that you need to cultivate. The guidelines that follow are reviewed in terms of 'do's' and 'don'ts', with no apology for any occasional repetition.

The Don'ts

You should **not**:

- be too clever: It is the argument that should win the reader round, not your flowery phrases, elegant quotations or clever approach.
- be too complicated: The point about simplicity has been made. It applies equally to the overall argument.
- be pompous: This means saying too much about you, your organization and your product/services/ideas (instead of what it means to the reader). It means writing in a way that is too far removed from the way you would speak. It means not following too slavishly the exact grammar at the expense of an easy, flowing style (though take care).
- over-claim: While you should certainly have the courage of your convictions, too many superlatives can become self-defeating. Make one claim that seems doubtful and the whole argument suffers. It ends up diluting your argument, annoying, reducing credibility and... Enough! Point made.
- offer opinions: Or at least not too many compared with statements of fact – ideally substantiated facts.
- lead into points with negatives: For example, do not say 'If this is not the case we will...' rather 'You will find... or...'
- assume your reader lacks knowledge: Rather than saying, for example, 'You probably do not know that...' it is better to say 'Many people have not yet heard...' or 'Like others, you probably know...'
- overdo humour: Never use humour unless you are very sure of it. An inward groan as they read does rather destroy the nodding agreement you are trying to build. I noticed a huge poster atop a high building near Bangkok airport,

which said that BMW was the 'torque of the town'. So clever, so funny – but for me, so yuk.

A quotation or quip, particularly if it is relevant, is safer and even if the humour is not appreciated, the appropriateness may be noted. I hope, incidentally, that this book makes you smile occasionally, but also that this intention is not overdone.

- use up benefits early: A persuasive case must not run out of steam: it must end on a high note and still be talking in terms of benefits even towards and at the end.

The Do's

You should **do** the following:

- concentrate on facts: The case you put over must be credible and factual. A clear-cut 'these are all the facts you need to know' approach tends to pay particular dividends
- use captions: For documents where this is relevant; while pictures, illustrations, photographs and charts can often be regarded as speaking for themselves, they will have more impact if used with a caption. (This can be a good way of achieving acceptable repetition, with a mention in the text and in the caption.)
- use repetition: Key points can appear more than once, for example in a leaflet and an accompanying letter, and even more than once within a letter itself. This applies, of course, especially to benefits repeated for emphasis.
- keep changing the language: Get yourself a thesaurus. You need to find numbers of ways of saying the same thing to create emphasis, for instance in linked documents like a brochure and an accompanying letter.
- say what is new: Assuming you have something new, novel – even unique – to say, make sure the reader knows it. Real differentiation can often be lost, so within the totality of a message make sure that the key points still stand out.
- address the recipient: You must do this accurately and precisely. You must know exactly to whom you are writing, what their needs, likes and dislikes are and be ever-conscious of tailoring the message. Going too far towards being all things to all people will dilute the effectiveness to any one recipient.
- keep them reading: Consider breaking sentences at the end of a page so that readers have to turn over to complete the sentence. (Yes, it does not look quite so neat, but it works.) Always make it clear that other pages follow, putting 'continued...' or similar at the foot of pages as necessary.

- link paragraphs: This is another way to keep people reading. Use 'horse and cart' points to carry the argument along. For example, one paragraph starts 'One example of this is...' the next starts 'Now let's look at how that works...'
- be descriptive: Be really descriptive! In words, a system may be better described as 'smooth as silk' rather than very straightforward to operate. Remember, you know how good 'the thing' you are describing is, the readers do not. You need to tell them and you must not assume they will catch your enthusiasm from a brief phrase.
- involve people: First your people. Do not say 'The Head of our XYZ Division', rather say 'John Smith, the Head of our XYZ Division'. And other people: do not say 'It is a proven service'... say 'More than 300 clients have found it valuable'.
- add credibility: For example, if you quote users, quote names (with their permission); if you quote figures, quote them specifically and mention people by name, 'Mary will check this for you'. Being specific adds to credibility, so do not say, 'This is described in our booklet on...' rather 'This is described on page 16 of our booklet on...'
- use repetition: Key points can appear more than once. This applies, of course, especially to benefits repeated for emphasis. You will notice this bullet point is repeated, either to show that the technique works or perhaps to demonstrate that I am pushing a half-hearted attempt at humour too far! If the latter, then it is not to be recommended.

EXAMPLES: PERSUASION WITHIN AND WITHOUT THE ORGANIZATION

Here we focus on two examples to illustrate some of the specific different circumstances in which persuasion is necessary.

These are:

1) an internal department-to-department communication; and
2) a letter to (potential) customers.

Internal persuasive communication

Consider a short scenario to set us up with an example.

John runs the sales office for a medium-sized company. His team is efficient. It comprises people who take customer enquiries, offer technical advice, handle queries of all kinds and take orders (a situation perhaps replaced in too many organizations by the ubiquitous call centre).

Recent reorganization has resulted in the merging of two departments. His people now occupy a large office together with another group: the order processing staff, people dealing with invoicing and documentation. For the most part, all is going smoothly. However, the routing of incoming telephone calls has become chaotic. The switchboard, despite having a note explaining who handles customers in which area of the country, is putting two out of three calls through to the wrong person, and the resulting confusion is upsetting staff and customers alike as calls have to be transferred.

John knows he must sort this out. He carefully drafts and sends a memo to the Personnel Manager, to whom the switchboard operators report, complaining that the inefficiency of their service is upsetting customers and putting the company at risk of losing orders. The memo he emailed is shown below:

> **From:** John B, Sales Office Manager
>
> **To:** Susan G, Personnel Manager
>
> **Subject:** Customer Service
>
> A recent analysis shows that, since the merging of the sales office and order processing department, two out of three incoming calls are being misrouted by the switchboard and have to be transferred.
>
> This wastes time and, more importantly, is seen by customers as inefficient. As the whole intention of this department is to hold and develop customer business by ensuring prompt, efficient service, this is not only a frustration internally, it risks reducing customers' image of the organization and, at worst, losing orders.
>
> I would be grateful if you could have a word with the supervisor and operators on the switchboard to ensure that the situation is rectified before serious damage results.

John is surprised to find that, far from the situation improving, all he gets is a defensive reply stating the total volume of calls with which the hard-pressed switchboard has to cope, and quoting other issues as being of far greater importance at present to the Personnel Department. It concludes by suggesting that he takes steps to ensure customers ask for the right person.

John intended to take prompt action that would improve customer service, he felt he had stated his case clearly and logically, yet all he succeeded in doing was rubbing a colleague up the wrong way. The problem remained.

Consider, for a moment, how else this might be handled before reading on. Why did it not work and cause resentment? And what might better have been said?

Here this initial communication was in writing. The email John sent, though well intentioned, had the wrong effect, and would also have made any follow-up conversation (necessary because the problem had still to be resolved) more difficult.

The problem is certainly identified in the email, the implications of it continuing are spelled out, and a solution – briefing of the relevant staff by the Personnel Manager – is suggested. The intention, as has been said, is good. However, despite a degree of politeness: 'I would be grateful...', the overall tone of the message is easy to read as a criticism. Further, the solution is vague, tell them what exactly? It seems to be leaving a great deal to Personnel. Maybe his opinion is 'it is not my fault, they should sort it out'. To an extent this may be true, but you may find you often have to choose between taking a line that draws attention to such a fact, or which sets out to get something done. These are often two different things, and the latter calls for a persuasive approach.

In this case the key objective is to change the action, and to do so quickly before customer relations are damaged. This is more important than having a dig at Personnel, and worth taking time to get the message exactly right. It is, while a matter of overall company concern, something of more immediate concern to the Sales Office.

COACHING SESSION 25

Internal persuasion

Before reading on, take a moment to draft a different version of this email, listing first your intentions and adding the actual text you believe will do a good job.

So what should John have done? You may well have sorted this in the last coaching session, but here's a suggestion. To ensure attention, collaboration and action, his message needed to:

- make the problem clear
- avoid undue criticism, or turning the matter into an emotive issue
- spell out a solution, or at least a suggestion of one
- make that solution easy and acceptable to people in Personnel (and, not least, the switchboard operators themselves).

Perhaps with that in mind, he should have written something more like the following:

> **From:** John B, Sales Office Manager
>
> **To:** Susan G, Personnel Manager
>
> **Subject:** Customer Service

The recent merger of the Sales Office and Order Processing Departments seems to have created some problems for the switchboard.

You will find that I have set out in this note something about what is happening and why, and offer specific suggestions to put it right. You will see the suggested action is mainly mine, but I would like to be sure that you approve before proceeding.

The problem

Since the merger, two out of every three incoming calls are misrouted and have to be transferred. This wastes time both in my department and on the switchboard, and is, of course, also likely to be seen as inefficient by customers. To preserve customer relations, and perhaps ultimately prevent orders being lost, the problem needs to be sorted out promptly.

The reason

Apart from the sheer volume of calls, always a problem at this time of the year, the problem is one of information. The switchboard operators have insufficient information to help guide them, and that which they do have has been outdated by the departmental merger. Given clear guidance neither they, nor customers, will have any problems.

Action

What I would suggest, therefore, are the following actions:

1. I have prepared a note (and map) showing which member of staff deals with customers from which geographical area, and would like to make this available for reference on the switchboard.

2. This might be best introduced at a short briefing meeting. If we could assemble the operators for ten minutes before the board opens one morning, I could go through it with them and answer any questions.
3. Longer term, it would be useful if the operators visited our department and saw something of what goes on, we could arrange a rota and do this over a few lunch hours so that it can be fitted in conveniently and without loss of productivity (we'll provide some sandwiches!).

If this seems a practical approach do let me know and I will put matters in hand.

This is not set out as the sole, 'correct' or guaranteed approach, but it is certainly different; and, I believe, better. And it seems to me to be more likely to work because it is designed specifically to be persuasive. Note especially that it:

- lays no blame
- recognizes that both Personnel, and the switchboard are important
- considers their needs for clear guidance, being able to handle the volume more easily, someone else taking the action
- anticipates objections; Personnel wondering who will do all this, for instance, and their not wanting any hassle
- is specific in terms of action. Who will do what and when (though maybe it could have specified the timing more precisely).

There seems every chance it will have the desired effect. Many situations exhibit similar characteristics. All it needs is a clear, systematic approach that recognizes the other person's point of view, and sells the desired solution and action.

External customer communication

We move on now to another before-and-after example, this time initiating sales contact. This letter is from a security company to the prospective new owner of a new-build house (addressed to me just before I moved). People moving house provide a good sales opportunity. People are often somewhat dilatory about security, but maybe the pleasure of a new house is likely to make thoughts of making it secure easier to sow.

The first letter is typical. But because it is introspective, features orientated, it contains too much unexplained jargon and formula 'officespeak', so it ends up selling itself short and makes an insufficient case out of what should be a strong one. It also has a really clichéd ending and leaves the initiative with the recipient to come back to them, rather than retaining the initiative.

Dear Mr Forsyth

I understand that you have bought the house on Plot 28 at Saltcote Maltings.

As part of their service the developer has retained us as advisors on all aspects of security including:

- intruder alarm systems
- security lighting
- closed circuit television
- entryphones
- any special security problems you may have.

I am writing to introduce my company and to offer our services in regard to security for your new home. We are dedicated to promoting and performing to high standards and to demonstrate our commitment, we:

- are members of British Security Industry Association
- have NACOSS (National Approval Council for Security Systems) certification
- adhere to BS4737 for equipment installation
- have ISO 9002 (quality management system) certification.

Enclosed are illustrations of typical robust and unobtrusive equipment we use. An alarm system would normally comprise a central control unit, keypad to set the system, PIRs (detection units), magnetic door contacts, alarm sounder and panic buttons.

You also have the option to enhance the protection and peace of mind provided by the system through connection to a central monitoring station. The monitoring station operates 24 hours a day, 365 days a year and can alert the police, a key-holder or anyone you specify. There are two options for connection to a central station – Red Care or Digital Communicator.

We can provide an annual maintenance and service contract which includes access to a 24 hour a day call-out service.

For further information please contact me on the above telephone number or complete and return the request form.

We assure you of prompt and diligent service.

Yours faithfully

As well as points referred to ahead of the letter, the punctuation and layout could perhaps be improved. So too could the clarity. The objective being set here is clearly to set up a meeting (on site).

COACHING SESSION 26

External persuasive communication

Here you may want to both critique the letter above, applying a red pen to the text, and also to rewrite it.

In the exercise above I am sure you found you could improve on the letter. If you want to compare your thinking with an example (again not the 'correct' solution) then I think something along the following lines would have made me think better of them – and made a response more likely.

Dear Mr Forsyth

28 Saltcote Maltings – keeping your new home safe

You must be excited about your planned move. It is a wonderful location which, as formal security advisors to the developer, we are getting to know well.

Sadly, any home may be vulnerable these days. And even a cursory glance at crime statistics gives us all pause for thought. No one wants the upset, loss, damage and feeling of fear a break-in produces; however, a little care can reduce risks dramatically.

What better time to check that security arrangements are satisfactory than as you move into a new home? You will want your house, possessions and family to be safe, and we can offer sound advice on how prudent action can make that so.

It may well be that even minor additions to the standard house specification can improve security significantly, and add a feeling of wellbeing. You can receive practical, expert advice – whether that is to fit just one more lock, or involving a full range of equipment: such as intruder alarms, security lights, entry phones or a full 24-hour monitoring service.

You will want to be sure any such advice is just that – sure.

We take our responsibilities, for both recommendation and installation, very seriously. We ensure we keep technically right up to date and are able to offer the best solutions to our customers through our membership of the British Security Industry Association; we also have NACOSS (National Approval Council for Security) certification and adhere to other quality standards.

Sound advice

Some of the equipment we use is described in the enclosed brochures. But our first concern is to identify and match your individual requirements, and recommend whatever suits you best.

You can arrange for a visit and discuss matters in principle without any commitment; we will never over-engineer the solution, and will only offer practical recommendations (not least to match your insurer's requirements). You can contact me at once and arrange a meeting; otherwise I will call you soon to see how we may be able to help.

Good security follows sound advice – and saying 'it will never happen to us', is really not one of the options.

Yours sincerely

P.S. Talk to us in good time – installation done as a new house is completed can ensure wiring is hidden and avoid mess after you move in.

Again this is, I think, better, both in terms of what it says and how it says it; the punctuation, readability and layout are better too. Both these letters were designed to be sent with brochures. It is impossible to illustrate a whole brochure here, though brochures are touched on in the next chapter.

A surprising number of documents in fact have some element of persuasion among their intentions. They will only act to prompt agreement if the case they put over is well designed to do just that.

The art of persuasion is a complex business. Accept that it is best described as helping people make decisions, then the individual techniques it involves are logical and common sense. The key issues are explored here.

In the next chapter we look at how the nature of a particular document affects how it should be written, taking a range of typical examples before focusing in more detail on emails and longer documents (such as reports and proposals) in the following two chapters.

TAKEAWAY

This section is designed to give you a moment to take stock. You may decide to read on, return to earlier coaching sessions or make some notes of progress to date and factors likely to be important to you in the future. Some notes in response to the questions here may prove useful as you proceed.

In what way and with whom must you be persuasive?

Are you absolutely clear on the distinction between benefits and features? (Double-check if there is any doubt.)

Should you return to the running example you have referred to in this chapter to check it in terms of an overall approach?

Similarly, are you clear about the need to bear the psychology of making decisions and how it must affect your own approach? Again you may want to refer back to your example.

6 HORSES FOR COURSES

OUTCOMES FROM THIS CHAPTER

- In this chapter we explore how writing must vary to fit its purpose and different types of communication method, review how to decide what is best in different circumstances and consider some examples as a basis for seeing how form and style must match purpose if what you write is to be effective.

WRITTEN OR NOT

It is said that words are chameleons – they reflect the colour of their environment. So here we investigate how writing must adapt to different types of document.

However, let's start with what may seem an odd question: but it's one with a message in mind – are you sure you should be writing? Not every message is best passed in writing. Do you think it is appropriate to hear that you have been made redundant (or better, promoted) in an email? Probably not.

Some messages are fine in writing. Others can need more than that: for example, a manager promoting someone might tell them in a one-to-one meeting, but confirm it in writing and send out news about it more widely so that others know what is going on.

Some messages may just be very difficult, or even impossible, to convey in written form.

COACHING SESSION 27

Unsuitable or impossible

Some things are not easy to convey in writing. Try telling someone how to tie a necktie? It is easy to show how, but in writing it is difficult. Have a try:

____

____

____

If you can think of any things in your working life area that present a similar problem then list them here; you may need to work on them or find other ways of putting over the information.

Mission impossible

The last coaching session might seem like a bit of fun, but the question it poses needs addressing. If something is difficult, or impossible, to explain or state clearly in writing then you may need to find another way, in whole or in part. This could range from adding a picture or diagram to considering a totally different way of communicating.

A SUITABLE MATCH

If you have decided that a written message is best, the next question is what will be appropriate? This is especially true of email.

Nothing has contributed more to a reduction in thought about how to communicate in writing than email. It is so easy to open your inbox and, faced with an onslaught of messages, dash off replies, only to discover later that what was sent was ill-considered. At worst this can get you into real trouble: something being misunderstood can cause problems – minor or major – and, at worst, something like an unthinkingly angry response can lead to a reprimand or even dismissal.

For the moment the moral is to take care; email has its own chapter in due course.

First, think, and then having decided on the communication method to be used, think again about the message you send and crucially what you write.

What you write will be influenced by certain factors relating to the form of work you do. There are of course innumerable possible examples, with just some discussed here.

The examples include:

- standard letters;
- chasing debtors;
- 'administrative' messages; and
- press releases.

Remember: any written business document must stand up to analysis; its major test is whether readers find it does the job it was intended to do. This means every document – however specialist or routine – must have a clear purpose and be understandable.

The examples here are not included in the form of templates to be slavishly copied. I believe that good writing comes from considering each document in its own right and building up your own good habits.

Certainly, there is no one right way to write anything. A variety of word combinations and styles can be appropriate, but there are some things that must be done in particular ways and there are certainly things to avoid.

STANDARD LETTERS

First example: consider the standard letter – the panacea for those not wanting to think about things?

Word processing is one of technology's wonderful gifts but there are also inherent dangers. Standard letters are a case in point.

Using such letters (and other documents for that matter) can save time and money and may speed up administration, customer service and more. They can be used to answer enquiries, queries or complaints or to follow up prospects; they save time in a big way, so far be it for me to suggest you do not use them. But if you do, then they better be good.

COACH'S TIP

Review date

It is very useful when you originate any new standard document to put a copy aside and allocate it a review date. Then check it a month or six months later or whenever appropriate to make sure it still sounds right – doing the job it was intended to do and doing it well.

A bad standard letter may go out, unthinkingly, hundreds of times and either fail to create understanding or, at worst, do actual damage – repeatedly. Remember the letter delivered under the hotel door mentioned early on: what it said was unclear and risked a poor image being created in a service business. Instead, standard letters should be:

- carefully created;
- reviewed regularly (they will not be suitable forever);
- given a sufficiently narrow focus (they cannot be all things to all people, and it is better to have three similar letters, each fitting slightly different situations, than one that fails to deliver in any situation);
- personalized, for example with a customer's name and details. This must always be correct; on a famous occasion a financial institution sent out thousands of promotional letters without adding the individual names, but left their internal description in place. They all arrived, addressed to 'Dear Rich Bastard';

- varied, at least a little, each time they are used (changing a few words or adding an additional sentence or paragraph is a small price to pay for getting the letter exactly right).

Inappropriately used standard letters are also a dead giveaway, spottable at 50 metres. And customers hate them.

COACH'S TIP

Just the job

Consider something else that may be important to you: your CV. There should be no such thing as a standard CV. They always need modifying to some degree depending on how they are used. This is to reflect the requirements of a particular job or organization to which they may be sent. Here the updating and editing of standard text can affect your whole career; so too for the covering letters you send with CVs. Taking note of this could one day change your life.

COACHING SESSION 28

Just your job

At the risk of this being a slight digression, it may be worth suggesting that you look at your own CV. Ask yourself: is it up to date and how does it read? Try this, say, once a year, whether you are likely to be seeking a new job or not (don't leave it too long since you will struggle to remember all the details).

If you conclude it needs revision then this may be a job to do separately, but by all means take a moment to make notes about possible revisions here.

CHASING DEBTORS

The next example has been included because of the awkwardness of writing such letters, which can blind the writer as to what actually needs to be done. One unforgettable example was a company that used eight standard letters to chase debts. These were sent progressively, and had an increasing tone of severity about them. They were ruined by the fact that each one had the same heading across the top in red – it said: 'Final demand'. Used over such a long sequence of letters actually created disbelief rather than credibility.

Such a letter must reflect firm policy. You decide what to do and state it clearly. A first letter may be no more than a reminder. Further down the line there is a need for increased firmness and you can only say what you truly intend to carry out.

If you say that in ten days the matter will be put in the hands of solicitors, then you must do just that. A lengthy reiteration of the basic request and then empty threats will achieve nothing.

Most people hate chasing overdue accounts, but remember the old maxim: 'It is not an order until the money is in the bank.' It is a job that must be done. I have heard of some bizarre ploys like sending a postcard, thus displaying the debt publicly (at least to the postman).

More appropriate is a systematic approach that follows up and follows up again. Ideally you need a fixed number of letters, all of which assume the matter has been overlooked accidentally, but lay down firm action. Such a sequence - here in three stages (though it could be more) - might go as follows. (Note: Words in brackets are comments, not part of the letters):

First reminder

Dear Xxxxxx

£1,550.98: overdue since (date)

You may recall receiving our invoice dated 27 November over a month ago itemizing the amount due for (state details and attach a copy).

I am writing to you because this payment is overdue. Perhaps it was simply overlooked, but I would appreciate payment being made promptly (adding details of how payment may be made). If there is any reason other than oversight why this has not been paid, please call (number) and ask to speak to Susan Jones who will be pleased to discuss the matter with you.

Yours

Second reminder

Dear Xxxxxx

£1,550.98: overdue since (date)

My accountant is now pressing me very hard to get this payment in. Very few customers seem to be as forgetful about payment as you appear to have been. Perhaps I may ask that a cheque is sent by return (again you may want to spell out alternative methods of payment, perhaps also restating the credit terms).

Prompt payment will save additional costs for us both, since I am now required to pass the matter over to a collection service if I do not hear from you, with your payment, within 7 days.

If there is any problem you want to discuss, please telephone (number) and ask to speak to Susan Jones who will make every effort to sort matters out.

Yours

Third reminder

Dear Xxxxxx

£1,550.98: collection arrangements

I have now written to you a number of times (you might specify) about this payment which dates from (date) when our invoice clearly specified 30 days' payment terms. As I have consistently received no reply, this matter is – as noted in my last letter – now being passed over to a collection service. This will quickly involve you in legal costs.

I do hope that you are able to respond immediately and prevent this. Payment may be made by (list methods).

Yours

The intention here is to be reasonable, clear and invoke the letter of the law (customers do surely understand that whatever they have contracted for must be paid for). At the end of the day you must draw a line, write no more and put the matter on a legal footing.

Note: Once a threat has been made and does not materialize, most bad payers will infer that the lack of assertiveness means that they have even longer to bolster their own cash flow situation.

Incidentally, this is not a task that can necessarily be exclusively carried out through correspondence. Other means of communication may also be involved typically in combination.

COACH'S TIP

A useful telephone tactic

If you do also have to telephone, don't make the call sitting at your desk but standing up. It may sound nonsense, but it works. It stops you saying: 'I'm sorry to worry you, but perhaps… ' and helps you sound far more assertive. If you do not believe it, try it!

Such letters emphasize the need for planning: what you need to achieve dictates the words you should use.

'ADMINISTRATIVE' LETTERS

Clearly there are thousands of things that could come under this heading. Many seem routine yet can still cause problems. Let us look at an example: a letter from a training organization to someone who failed to attend a programme on the date on which they were booked and who wrote requesting a refund.

In such a situation, a too formal or an off-hand approach can lead to letters that do more harm than good – as with this example.

> (heading)
>
> 15 March 2015
>
> Peter Smith
>
> Clocktower Engineering Ltd
>
> Arlton Road
>
> London N1
>
> Dear Mr Smith
>
> Thank you for your letter of 14 March. You will see that you missed attending our training programme 'Making Successful Presentations', which you were registered to attend on 10 March because you misread the joining instructions.
>
> The enclosed copy clearly shows that the correct details of time and place were sent to you.
>
> If you want to try again, the programme runs again next month on 22 April, at the same venue. You will need to record your intention to attend in writing.
>
> Yours sincerely
>
> John Nickson

This may be accurate, but it is abrupt and impolite and neither helpful nor likely to win friends and influence people.

COACHING SESSION 29

Clear, appropriate routine

Try planning and rewriting the letter here.

Again, without claiming this is perfect or the only right way, how about something along the following lines?

(heading)

15 March 2015

Peter Smith

Clocktower Engineering Ltd

Arlton Road

London N1

Dear Mr Smith

Seminar booking for 10 March:

'Making Successful Presentations'

No doubt you were annoyed to miss the above seminar for which you were registered as a delegate; I was sorry to receive your letter of 14 March setting out the circumstances.

While the joining instructions (copy enclosed) sent to you did give the correct information, given the short notice on attendance we perhaps should have made the details clearer. My apologies.

Luckily the programme is scheduled to run again before too long. I have therefore moved your registration forward to the next date – 22 April. It is at the same venue. I hope you will find this convenient and be able to put the date in your diary now while places remain available. Information about this (and about later dates, just in case) is enclosed.

My secretary, Sue, will telephone you in a day or two to see if this suits. Meantime, I am sure you will find the programme useful when you do attend – if you have any special objectives in attending do let us know; we aim to meet participants' needs as individually as possible.

I look forward to meeting you next month.

Yours sincerely

John Nickson

Better? I think so. Though this example relates only to a simple confusion – by the client – the approach, letting the reader down gently and still offering convenient alternative action, is better and the difference between the two letters is clear.

WRITING A PRESS RELEASE

Certain documents need a special approach because of the way they are regarded within the business world and how they are usually experienced. Where such a convention exists it is worth following it, not slavishly necessarily, but carefully – especially when it is the recipients who dictate the format.

So, the final example in this chapter we consider press releases. Press relations is an important part of the broader technique of public relations (both confusingly abbreviated to PR).

An important element of communication with the media is the issuing of **press releases**: these are precisely written communications designed to prompt a mention of something that can be described as news about an organization in various media. They are also referred to as news releases.

Press releases demand that certain conventions are complied with; at least editors will pay more attention to them if they do so. These are spelled out below, together with an example of a press release. Again, you should not follow this slavishly: remember that an element of creativity is always necessary and the overriding idea is to ring bells and differentiate each message from those of others competing for the same space.

COACH'S TIP

Not too much

Do not 'cry wolf'. Save press releases for when you really have a story. If you send a series of contrived releases, there is a danger that a good one among them will be ignored.

There are two – perhaps contradictory – aspects of putting together a press release that will stand a good chance of prompting press mentions. The first is to comply with the 'form' demanded by the newspapers, magazines and other media to whom releases are sent; the second is to differentiate what you say so that it stands out as being of genuine interest from the very large number of releases received.

The details of composing an effective press release are set out here, checklist style.

Consider the 'form' first.

- It should carry the words 'Press (or News) Release' at the top, together with the date, preferably at the top left-hand side of the first page.
- If an embargo is necessary (i.e. a request not to publish before a certain date, to ensure news appears as near as possible simultaneously – as once an item has been in print others will consider it of less interest), it should be clearly stated 'EMBARGO: not to be published before (time) on (date)'. Use CAPITALS or **bold type** for emphasis.

Learn in a week, what the experts learn in a lifetime

Apply the secrets of the experts and learn quickly with the Teach Yourself *In A Week* series. This acclaimed series provides you with the tools to get on the fast track to success. With authoritative instruction from expert authors, the highly practical *In A Week* will help you to progress in your career and master specific problems. Structured into 7 easily-adopted daily chapters, you'll be motivated and able to learn on the go.

OUTSTANDING CONFIDENCE
IN A WEEK

By Patrick Forsyth
Bestselling author and trainer

The ability to maintain confidence is crucial to anyone who wants to advance their career.

Written by Patrick Forsyth, leading expert and coach in confidence-building techniques, this book quickly teaches you the insider secrets you need to know to in order to gain outstanding confidence.

The highly motivational 'in a week' structure of the book provides seven straightforward chapters explaining the key points, and at the end there are optional questions to ensure you have taken it all in. There are also cartoons and diagrams throughout, to help make this book a more enjoyable and effective learning experience.

Sunday: What is confidence?
Monday: Self analysis
Tuesday: The nature of the work place
Wednesday: Working at creating confidence
Thursday: The contribution of appearance
Friday: Communications to the rescue
Saturday: A foundation of knowledge and skill

Outstanding Confidence in a Week is an invaluable tool to help fast track you to success. So what are you waiting for?

To request a review copy, an interview with the authors or for further information please contact XXXs, email: XXXs, or tel: XXXs.

Join the conversation:
www.inaweek.co.uk
Linkedin: Teach Yourself In A Week Practical

- Also, at the top you need a heading, not too long but long enough to indicate clearly the contents of the release or to generate interest in it.
- Space text out well with wide margins, reasonable gaps between paragraphs and so on. This allows recipients to make notes on it.
- If it runs to more than one page, make sure it says 'continued', or similar, at the foot of each page, even breaking a sentence at the end of the page will make it more likely that people will turn over.
- Similarly, to make it absolutely clear that there is no more, many put 'end' at the foot of the last page.
- Use newspaper style. Short paragraphs. Short sentences. Two short words rather than one long one.
- Keep it brief, long enough to put over the message and onto a second page if necessary, but no more.
- The first sentences are crucial and need to summarize as far as possible the total message.
- Avoid overt 'plugging' (although that may well be what you are doing). Do not mention names etc. right at the beginning, for example.
- Try to stick to facts rather than opinions. An accountant saying: 'This event is being arranged for all those who are interested in minimizing their tax liability', for example, is better than 'This event will be of great interest to all those wanting to minimize their tax liability'.
- Opinions can be given, in quotes, and ascribed to an individual. This works well and can be linked to the attachment of a photograph (which should usually be attached as a print and clearly labelled in case it gets separated from the release, but also with clear indications as to how an electronic version can be emailed).
- Do not overdo the use of adjectives, which can jeopardize credibility.
- Avoid underlining things in the text since this is used as an instruction in printing to put words underlined in italics.
- Separate notes from the text as footnotes, for example, 'photographers will be welcome'; they could get printed as part of the story.
- Never omit from a release, at the end, a clear indication of where further information can be sought. Provide name(s), telephone number(s), email address(es) and so on.
- Make sure finally that it is neat, cleanly typed and presentable and that it lists any/all enclosures/attachments. This last point may be obvious perhaps, but important.

So, how do you make your press release stand out? Make sure the story sounds interesting and, without overdoing things, be enthusiastic about it. If you are not, why should they be? Perhaps the only good thing in the world that is contagious is enthusiasm. A press release should infect someone else with your own enthusiasm (though some releases are there intentionally to flag bad news. For example, if an organization is downsizing then it may need to say so to prevent rumour and exaggeration).

To show an example here I have used the release sent out by the publishers of this book for an earlier title I wrote in their 'In A Week' series. If this does not reflect everything I have said, then it just goes to show that none of this is an exact science; judgement is always required to settle the final form of any document.

COACHING SESSION 30

Press release

If writing press releases is something you must do (or would like to experiment with), then take time to draft one here about some news relating to your own organization.

A CREATIVE TOUCH

As a final thought, and as a plea to consider approaching business writing creatively, consider this:

Sometimes something special is needed to make a powerful impression. A good example of this is the second or third communication in a sequence aiming to chase something down, perhaps aiming to prompt agreement from a boss or a customer. Such messages, typically a letter or email, are perhaps difficult to compose because you may feel that your best shot has been sent and you are wondering 'What can I say next?' Such follow-up communications can:

- repeat key issues (but must find a different way to put at least some of the message).
- simply remind (with strong contacts this may be all that is necessary).
- offer different action. (For instance, the first communication to a customer says: Buy it, the second says: let us show you a sample, or finds some more novel way of continuing the dialogue).

The only option

Sometimes there is little new left to say (simply, 'it's me again'), especially if the proposition is good and the only reason for lack of confirmation is timing or distraction rather than that the recipient is totally unconvinced and more persuasion is necessary. In which case the job is to continue to maintain contact, and ultimately to jog them into action; and one reaches a point when appearing distinctive or memorable – and perhaps somewhat un-business-like-writing – is the only remaining option (as the example below shows).

The example that follows illustrates what I mean by un-business-like-writing.

After writing a short book for a specialist publisher, I was keen to undertake something on another topic for them in the same unique format. The proposal got a generally good reaction, but no confirmation was forthcoming. I wrote and telephoned a number of times. Nothing positive materialized – there was always a delay or a put-off (you may know the feeling!).

A final further message needed to be sent (rather than give up and perhaps let the moment pass); all the conventional possibilities seemed to have been exhausted. Realizing that, I wrote and sent the following brief message modelled on an old-style lonely hearts advertisement.

'Struggling author, patient, reliable (non-smoker), seeks commission on business topics. Novel formats preferred, but anything considered within reason. Ideally 100 or so pages, on a topic like sales excellence sounds good; maybe with some illustrations. Delivery of the right quantity of material – on time – guaranteed. Contact me at the above address/telephone number or let's meet on neutral ground, carrying a copy of *Publishing News* and wearing a carnation.'

Despite some initial hesitation, wondering if it was too informal or over the top (I was proposing to send it to someone I had only met once), I went ahead. I did so on headed paper and by post, feeling that this would have more impact than an email. Gratifyingly, the approach was appreciated and confirmation came the following day (and you can now read the result – *The Sales Excellence Pocketbook*: Management Pocketbooks).

Similarly, the example given in Chapter four about the report of a research study (describing the organization with the phrase 'an old sofa') makes the same point. Both might never have been sent; yet both worked very well.

I wonder how many times similar missives are deleted to the tune of sucking of teeth and a 'not really what I can say' aside, when being a little more bold might work much better.

Sometimes a slightly less conventional approach – and some seemingly non-business writing language – does work well. Try a little experiment and see what it can do for you.

COACHING SESSION 31

A creative touch

See if there is a place among the examples of your own work for something, let's say, 'unconventional'. If so, whether it is a page or just a paragraph, have a go at writing in a more creative, novel style than your normal inclination – and see if you can come up with something you feel works.

NEXT STEPS

The point is made strongly here that your writing needs to be matched to the individual circumstance: the recipient and the communications method used. Various examples have been given and the points made have general relevance too. But two kinds of document need more lengthy review: the first is email – that 'can't live without it, but hate it too' method that is so prevalent in the workplace. This we look at in the next chapter, with longer documents, such as reports, being the subject of the following chapter.

TAKEAWAY

This section is designed to give you a moment to take stock. You may decide to read on, return to earlier coaching sessions or make some notes of progress to date and factors likely to be important to you in the future. Some notes in response to the questions here may prove useful as you proceed.

1. Can you think of anything you are writing about that would be better conveyed by some other communications method (or a combination of them) and if so what might be better?

2. Are any standard letters (or documents) you use likely, on reflection, to need amending/updating? Be honest here and, if so, what action does this demand?

3. Is your approach to the routine too routine in style and tone and, if so, how might it be changed for the better?

4. Do you ever actively prevent yourself writing as creatively as you usefully might and, if so, should you change a habit?

7 THE UBIQUITOUS EMAIL

OUTCOMES FROM THIS CHAPTER

- Email has become so important and so much used that it inevitably needs its own chapter. Here we review the special nature of email communications (and also how to avoid its hazards), before going on to look at tips and techniques for writing effective emails and doing so while managing your time efficiently.

THE NATURE OF EMAIL

Email is one of the quickest ways of communicating with other people, instantly sending as it does letters, memos, pictures and sounds from one computer to another via the Internet on a worldwide basis. The technicalities do not need to concern us here; but the communications implications do.

In the workplace, email is often used as a substitute for other kinds of communication, reducing the need for face-to-face meetings. This can be useful: it is possible to conduct meetings, correspond across the whole world and use voice and visual contact without leaving your desk.

However, the use of email can be overdone, reducing personal contact to the detriment of relationships and collaboration. It is important to have a balance in terms of different forms of contact. Some organizations have adopted rules to counter any negative effects, say 'No internal emails are to be sent on a Thursday.'

Because emailing is rapid, it brings pressure on the individual responsible for creating the emails to get them right first time in terms of passing on a clear message; there is a tendency to dash them off, which must be resisted as a poorly written one can cause misunderstanding, or worse (I am sure that you can think of examples, perhaps all too easily!).

COACH'S TIP

Suspend reaction – use the 5-minute rule

It is often wise to delay sending a hastily written email for five minutes (or more!) before pressing the 'send' button. If you are angry or upset when you write something, it is a good idea either to take a break or go for a walk or do something else, before writing, certainly before sending. Even if you write a message once you have cooled off, it pays to take a moment to review it before sending it out.

COACHING SESSION 32

Your inbox

As a first illustration of the importance of email, and how it differs from other forms of communication, you can do worse than look at your own inbox. Pick a period, say a month or two back in your record and look at 20–30 consecutive messages. If you ask the following questions (and record the answers) it will tell you something, and perhaps be a sobering experience.

- How many out of the total were important at the time?

____

____

____

____

- What proportion made complete sense and told you all you wanted/needed to know?

____

____

____

____

- What proportion do you still need to keep for the record?

____

____

____

____

It is likely that your analysis will show you both how useful yet how potentially time-wasting email can be. Keep this in mind as you read on.

The main attractiveness of email is without doubt its speed. Mail is sent immediately you click the 'Send' button; the speed of reply down to how quickly someone checks their inbox and replies. The fast to and fro nature of email communication can prompt rapid action and boost efficiency.

Technology is not infallible

It may be worth bearing in mind that despite the wonders of the technology, a small proportion of emails do go astray and fail to arrive. Asking for acknowledgement of your most important emails may therefore be sensible (and you can do this via an automatic request if you wish).

EMAIL VERSUS SNAIL MAIL

The writing of an email can be, indeed usually is, less formal than writing a letter.

Let's say this firmly and up front. The level of formality must be selected wisely. There are those to whom you may write very informally (incorporating as many abbreviations, grammatical shortcuts, minimal punctuation and bizarre spellings as you wish) as long as your meaning is clear. But others (customers, senior colleagues) may resent this or think worse of you for it.

Sometimes (usually?) an email must be as well written as any important letter. It is safest to adopt a fairly formal style, and certainly a clear one, and err on the side of more rather than less formality if you are unsure. Proofreading is as important here as with many other documents.

Email's main purpose is not for lengthy communications but usually for short, direct information-giving or -gathering. Lengthy emails are difficult to read and absorb on screen. For this and other reasons, different means of communication are sometimes better options.

When replying to an email, you don't have to worry about finding the sender's name and address and job title. Responding only involves the pressing of a 'reply' button.

Here's one example of what is possible: a company located in Wisconsin, US, emailed its service consultants in Cambridge, UK about obtaining a specific part for a processing machine. The UK office emailed the manufacturers in Manila, Philippines for information. They responded by email within minutes. The reply was then transmitted back to the US company. Total time taken – 17 minutes for a message from Cambridge to reach around the world and fulfil an order.

Possible disadvantages?

There are downsides, however, for instance:

- Email agreement is just as legally binding as a formal document; treating it otherwise can cause problems.
- If technical issues put your system out of action this can cause problems; and technical back-up needs to be in place fast to avoid problems.
- Junk email – or 'spam' – is just as irritating as the junk mail that arrives through the letterbox. It is sensible to reduce its time-wasting volume – and dangers – by having, and keeping up to date, software that isolates it (within an organization this may mean liaising with the IT department).
- Caution should be exercised in opening emails and attachments from unknown recipients as viruses, Trojan horses and worms can invade a computer system if care is not taken. We will return to this later.

COACH'S TIP

A personal matter

Other potential problems include people sending personal messages that can waste much time in an organization. If it is done on a company heading or format there may be legal implications, too. What happens if something is libellous? Thus, organizations need firm policy guidelines and the individual needs to be disciplined in exercising care in this respect.

THE BASICS

Emails can be more informal than letters but still certain rules as regards style and content are sensible. Given the volume of emails people receive, you are competing for attention and must compose emails that are effective. An email should always aim to be:

- **succinct** – use plain words and keep it brief
- **direct** – clear presentation, no ambiguity
- **logical** – with a clear structure.

Whether emails are being sent internally or externally, as a substitute for a letter or not, it is important to ensure these rules are observed. A clear heading will make the purpose of your message apparent and it may also be helpful to flag any (real!) urgency and say whether, and perhaps when, a reply is sought. Remember that email can, like any communication have many intentions – to inform, persuade, etc.

Split second

It is said that the definition of a split second is the amount of time taken by someone deciding that a message is irrelevant and their pressing 'Delete'. One overriding reason for taking care and writing good and appropriate emails is that unless they are quickly recognized as significant – they may be gone!

GETTING ORGANIZED

Because of their popularity and versatility, emails currently threaten to obliterate all other forms of communication. It is vital to stay on top of them, so:

- try to clear your inbox every day, replying as appropriate
- categorize items that are time critical and items that will require work later
- delete any emails that are irrelevant or unimportant
- unsubscribing from email lists assists in clearing the clutter in your inbox
- copy yourself (cc) or blind copy (bcc) yourself a message when responding to emails where arranging a meeting or promising a response or sending information
- ration the reading of emails to, say, three times a day, early morning, midday and end of day. Reading messages as soon as they flash on the screen causes severe interruptions
- delete messages that you've dealt with and empty the deleted folder regularly
- when replying to messages where your reply is integrated into the original text, make sure that the responses you insert are in a different colour to draw attention to revisions and insertions.

Make no mistake, being disorganized can compound the problem of it being all too easy to dash things off and then be less than effective.

COACHING SESSION 33

Check your level of organization

Set out your current practice in terms of when you do what to keep your email well organized. Add a list of things that make your emailing more effective and ensure these points become habitual.

Use the following checklist as a prompt to good practice.

Do not:

- send emails just because they are easy
- enter text IN CAPITAL LETTERS. It is regarded as shouting and may be taken as rude
- use them as a substitute for properly delegating a task to another
- send them to discharge yourself of responsibility
- write something in an email that is confidential
- forward someone's email without their permission
- assume your recipient wanted it and is desperate to receive it.

Do:

- think and use the 'send later' button to inject some thinking time
- be precise in order to eliminate follow-up checks, phone calls, etc.
- reply promptly. Because email is quick, a reply is generally expected sooner rather than later (it may be worth exchanging your practice with regular correspondents so that both parties are aware of how the other works)
- be polite and friendly but never assume familiarity with your jargon
- keep attachments to a minimum and make clear what they are (your personal file description may not be suitably explanatory to others)
- avoid gobbledygook.

COACH'S TIP

Add paper

The paperless office predicted a while ago seems to be taking time to arrive. Realistically some messages need paper copies, so it is a useful habit to print out emails that need to go into files or reminder systems as soon as you deal with them. Leave it even a short time and you can find the message has disappeared below the visible screen and is effectively lost.

THINK BEFOREHAND

Like so much else, emails are made better by the simple act of engaging the brain before your typing fingers. Consider the following to help ensure that emails are presented effectively:

1. What is the **objective** or purpose of an email?

   Do you know what you are trying to achieve? Is the email a request for information? Are you circulating standard information? If the email is a quick response to a query, make sure that what you say is correct.

   If you are unsure, explain that this is an acknowledgement of receipt, and you will come back to them as soon as you can or, better, specify when this will be. If you do not know what the objective is, think carefully before sending your communication.

2. What is the **background** to the issue?

   Is the reason for sending the email something that is to do with a problem in a project? Is there an explanation, excuse or apology required? Is it to elicit more information or to provide detailed answers to a query?

   For an email to be clearly understood, there must be a reason why you are sending it. If you find that you don't know what this is, check and think before writing.

3. Who is the intended **recipient**?

   Will it reach them directly, or be read by another person? Email inboxes are not necessarily only opened by the person named in the 'Send to' box. It is possible that colleagues have access to a person's mailbox, for example when someone is sick or on holiday.

   It is important to bear this in mind when writing a message in case of problems.

4. What **style** are you using?

   How is it being presented? Is the style at a suitable level of formality? Are you replying to a message that was half-encrypted with lots of missing capital letters, text message style shortened words, emoticons, etc.?

   If so, that is fine. But think carefully about what impression the style of the email gives to someone who is opening a communication from you for the first time.

5. Choice of **content**.

   What is the email saying and is it being clearly communicated without any vagueness and ambiguity?

   If the email covers complex matters, it may be better to explain that a document containing details follows. Emails are usually intended to be read quickly, and the content should reflect this.

6. Is there a **conclusion**/recommendation/response required?

   If so, is it obvious? It may be clearer to place any request for action at the end of the email. Also, by saying something like, 'it would be helpful if you could bring this information with you when we meet at 4pm', you give the recipient a clear message that they have until 4pm to complete the task.

   Finishing off an email with a direct instruction/request, or repeating the purpose of the message, will leave the reader in no doubt about what your intention is.

7. What, if any, **attachments** are being sent?

   Specify any attachments clearly. If the attachments require certain software to open them, explain what is needed. This is particularly important where graphics and images are being sent. Some of these attachments can take ages to download and it is helpful to say so.

COACHING SESSION 34

Analysing your own email style

Consider the seven points just reviewed and again select a relatively long email at random and analyse it – noting how well its composition addresses the issues mentioned.

1. ______________________________

2. ______________________________

3. ______________________________

4.

5.

6.

7.

FURTHER DETAILED CONSIDERATIONS

Putting yourself across appropriately in an email is important, because it is instant and non-retrievable. As with other written communication, there is no tone of voice, facial expression, posture, body language and gestures to augment your message; only the words convey your meaning. As email is a rapid and concise form of communication, the detail matters.

Checklist

These are some of the most important points of detail to remember if you are to achieve precision and thus understanding and a chance of your objectives being met:

- Format – Use an appropriate format or house style – this is often available as a template. Make sure it matches the style used in the organization's letters and check what other aspects of layout are expected to conform.
- Typography/font – Most companies have a prescribed font and style but others can be chosen from the drop-down list box. The screen shows the font and size selected. You can also elect to highlight text in your email, using devices such as bold, underline or italic.
- Subject – writer reference, case number or project name. This is just a polite way of ensuring that the recipient can save time by reading what the email refers to. If you are sending an email to someone about a particular matter, it is helpful if they understand immediately what the message is about. One problem occurs if the correspondence goes to and fro and the subject is not changed/updated and ceases to be clear. Take care with this.
- Salutation – Are you on first name terms? Do you need to write in a more formal style because you have not exchanged correspondence before? Pick the most appropriate style of address.
- Punctuation – Beware ambiguity. A missing comma or no full stop can often cause confusion. It may be 'cool' to lose capitals and miss out 'dots and dashes' but if the reader is left puzzled by the meaning, you are less likely to get a useful exchange of information.
- Line length – Short sentences and line length make for easier reading on screen. This is explained in more detail further on. Do not use complex sentences or syntax. Short and sweet is best.
- Paragraphing – Options are available from the drop-down list, including headings, bulleted and numbered lists. Paragraphing should be used where there is a change of topic or subject, so that the reader is aware that a new point is being introduced.

- Consistency – If the email contains numbering take care. It is extremely irritating if the numbering changes in style or is inconsistent. If you are making a number of points, stick to a), b), c) sequence or 1.i, 1.ii, 1.iii or whatever style or format you prefer.
- Valediction – Unlike a formal letter you don't have to sign off 'yours faithfully' or 'yours sincerely', however in some cases it may be appropriate to end with an informal send off. Many people use 'kind regards', 'many thanks' and 'best wishes' or more impersonally, 'yours'. This can be part of a signature (see below).
- Writer details – title, organization. With emails it is possible to set up as a 'default' a signature (or signatures) that appear at the foot of the message. It can include your name and title as well as details of any organization you represent.
- Contact details – These go with signature and should include any contact details necessary – like those that appear on your letterhead (address, telephone, website, etc.).
- Attachments – As mentioned before, these should be clearly described and referred to in the text.

Note: While the points made here are especially important in context of the special nature of email, they overlap with the general principles of what makes any written message effective.

TIME-WASTING EMAILS

Junk emails are a nuisance and can be time-consuming to keep on top of. Emails received from reputable bodies sending legitimate commercial email, as compared to 'illegal spammers' are within the law. The majority of illegal spam emails can be readily identified from the address and/or subject and immediately deleted without being opened.

Anti-spam filters are incorporated into most mail/computer systems. They are not guaranteed to catch everything, but they certainly reduce the volume of spam reaching inboxes. Get one and use it both to block items that you know you don't want (unwanted circulars, for instance) and to stop things that 'seemingly' come out of the blue.

Beware of opening messages from unidentifiable sources, and never open an attachment from an unknown source. These can contain viruses or micro-programs that can access your information and send it to others. Also remember that replying to illegal spam will often make things worse. The spammer will know that the email address is valid, will continue to use it and circulate it to other spammers.

Security

This is an area to be vigilant about – the pitfalls are too many to go into here but you should be familiar with, and use, all appropriate security devices (for example you may need to check out electronic signatures or even encryption. Not doing so can waste untold amounts of time. Enough. You have been warned!

THE ROLE OF LANGUAGE

The lack of formality of many email messages has previously been mentioned. But clarity is essential and many messages must look and sound good and over-informality is a danger. So, remember:

- to spellcheck your emails when necessary. Be aware of easily confused words and use 'spellcheck' with caution. As an example of the dangers, consider a message saying, 'After further consideration I have decided that your request for a salary increase of £10,000 per annum will now be agreed' Try that sentence again inserting the word 'not' instead of 'now'.
- use grammar and language checks and such features as the thesaurus: all can help you to produce an effective message. It is possible to select alternative words or phrases to avoid confusion when using the grammar check tool.
- **Note:** You may want to check again the section about language and the avoidance of such issues as tautology (e.g. the nonsense of 'new innovation').

Grammatical errors make an essentially simple email unwieldy and less likely to do a good job.

Jargon and acronyms

It has been said that you need a degree in abbreviations to read emails.

Emails containing jargon, text language and acronyms (where initial letters from phrases are used to make up another word) can easily be confusing. However, because of email's overriding informality it is a good idea to be familiar with those that are universally used. There are many around and new ones are springing up daily due to the popularity of text messaging. Here is a selection of some of the more common such abbreviations that you are likely to see in emails:

FYI For your information

AFAIK As far as I know

BCNU Be seeing you

BTW By the way

CUL8R See you later

TNX Thanks

COACH'S TIP

A bit of DNA*

It would be a good idea to learn certain appropriate abbreviations, especially ones that are commonly used within your organization, profession or industry sector. Beware using them in emails that are being sent outside the firm where the recipient does not understand them. When using acronyms or any abbreviations, do not assume others will understand; it is courteous to use full terminology in parenthesis afterwards.

*Do not assume

ATTACHMENTS

Email is made infinitely more useful because documents and files can be attached to them. Attachments can include word-processed documents, images, audio or video files. It is even possible to email computer programs.

When an attachment is sent the email program copies the file from where it is located and attaches it to the message. Image files can take some time to upload and download, so it is advisable to keep these to a minimum if speed is of the essence.

It may help to compress files that are being sent as email attachments. This will reduce the upload time while transmitting the information. It also speeds up the download time for you if someone sends you a large file that has already been zipped. 'Zip' and 'Stuff it' are well-known programs and Microsoft Windows includes a compression tool.

The advantage of sending documents and files as attachments is the speed and efficiency of communications. The recipient of the documents will be able to keep these on file and can edit, return or forward them on as necessary.

If preserving integrity is an issue, an attachment should be sent in PDF format (Print Document File). This is very safe and secure for sensitive material (though there are, unsurprisingly, ways round it).

HYPERLINKS

Inserting hyperlinks into email messages is particularly useful when sending information to people; these allow you to flag a specific web page to someone and for them to open it and see it with a single click.

Remember that some people may not bother and then the information sent this way as a part of a total message might thus never be seen and dilute the whole effect.

COACH'S TIP

Your profile

Always remember that you cannot tell who will read your emails, either immediately or in the future. You can tell a lot about a person from their email style (and by reading between the lines), and it can provide a window to someone's status in the workplace, competence, work habits, stress levels and even their personality. You must pick carefully the level of formality you adopt and may conclude that you need to minimize the use of cheeky quotes, smiley faces – emoticons – or (groan-making) joke mails.

TOP TIPS

Emails are such a valuable communication tool for so many of us, but if abused or used carelessly, can cause trouble. So, in summary, and in order to emphasize the need for attention to detail, here are eight basic tips for better email technique.

1. **Use email as one channel of communication in your armoury, but not the only one.**

   Do not become lazy just because email is fast and easy. Emails can document discussions and send high impact messages around the world at the click of a mouse. But they can also mislead; for example, managers sometimes think they can communicate with large groups of people *solely* through regular group emails.

   Use email widely but not as an exclusive management tool. It is not possible to reach everyone, and the impersonal, non-direct contact means that people can feel slighted by the loss of any personal touch.

2. **It pays to keep it short and sweet.**

   Emails that are longer than a full screen tend not to be read straightaway. They get left till later and often not until the end of the day or the following morning

It is important to judge when it is right to put down the mouse and seek out the person for a face-to-face meeting, or pick up the phone and speak to them.

Overuse of email can actually erode time effectiveness unnecessarily.

3. **Be clear – always.**

   Email requires clarity of purpose. Be sure your message comes across without any ambiguity and the confusion that can follow it. Also, it is important to be sure to whom your message needs to be addressed, and who needs to be copied in for information. In terms of actions and priorities, use lists or bullet points for clarity. Response buttons (or similar) should be used if you need to see who has received and read your message.

4. **Encourage open communication.**

   Request that recipients respond with questions or queries if they wish. It shows that you are concerned and available to help.

5. **Do not use emails to get angry with people.**

   Far better to save anger for face-to-face encounters (if it is appropriate at all) where facial expression and body language can be used to great effect, or over the phone where tone of voice can speak volumes.

   Sarcasm, irony, criticism or venom is not appropriate when sending emails. Such feelings can often come over far more harshly than intended.

6. **Humour should be used with caution.**

   By all means use wit and humour to lighten a heavy atmosphere but emoticons, smiley faces and joke mails are rarely appropriate in the work environment. If being facetious is usual for you, it may make it more difficult to strike a serious note when you need to. Some companies ban joke emails; they are too risky. Too many joke emails erode your attempts to send serious ones.

7. **Set aside time to deal with emails.**

   Because of the growing importance of emails, you need to make time to deal with them; if this demands reconfiguring your working day – so be it.

8. **Take advantage of tools such as spellcheck and thesaurus.**

   To avoid errors and complicated sentences, use the tools provided to ensure clarity of communication. If you are unsure whether something works, check by asking a friend or colleague.

Next time you send an email, double-check it against the principles set out in this chapter to make sure it is effective.

COACHING SESSION 35

A test email

This would be a good moment to write an email while the ideas reviewed here are fresh in your mind. Since emails arrive, for most people, regularly and in some quantity, it should be possible to go to your inbox and find one needing a reply to use as a test. Preferably pick something that needs more than just a line or two.

Write your reply here first and check it against the thoughts in this chapter before typing and sending it. Note: Your example does not need to be a reply – there may be something you plan to send that can equally make a good example if you wish. Or why not try both?

COACH'S TIP

Copies

Do not send copies to all and sundry – this is a prime cause of the over-proliferation of email and many are unnecessary; ask (demand?) to be dropped off unnecessary circulation lists.

NEXT STEPS

Here we have explored a comparatively recent type of communication, albeit one that has become the most prolific. It can present its own problems and, as we have seen, needs care since the methodology seems to encourage carelessness hand in hand with providing speed.

Next we turn from a category that includes perhaps the shortest possible documents to look at longer ones requiring the writing of a far greater quantity of words.

TAKEAWAY

This section is designed to give you a moment to take stock. You may decide to read on, return to earlier coaching sessions or make some notes of progress to date and factors likely to be important to you in the future. Some notes in response to the questions here may prove useful as you proceed.

Is the way you use your email well-organized or is this something you should check/adjust?

Do you – be honest – have a tendency to dash off some of your email communications in a way that risks misunderstanding or worse, and if so what habits can you adopt to prevent this?

Is your style always well matched to the individual situation/recipient and, again, if not, what action should you resolve to take?

Additionally, is your style sufficiently distinctive and is it likely to make recipients welcome hearing from you? If not, think about adjustments.

8

WRITING LONG DOCUMENTS

OUTCOMES FROM THIS CHAPTER

- In this chapter we review lengthy texts and explore how to create a structure for such documents, how to write to match their nature and purpose and how to present them to make a positive impression and maximize the likelihood of their achieving their aims.

A few people baulk at writing a note for the milkman, some people might regard long as anything more than 2 or 3 pages, while others might reserve this description for report-type documents of 10, 20 pages or more.

Long documents present their own problems. Even this book! It may be some 50,000 words, but it is divided into a number of chapters and each of those addresses numerous issues and is in turn broken down into a number of sections. If one regards each as an entity, then at one level there is rarely more than 3,000 or 4,000 words to consider together.

Of course, the overall content needs planning and organizing, but with a plan in mind then the writing falls mainly into bite-sized sections. So too does a report, proposal or any other business document. By taking this approach all lengthy writing is possible.

WRITE TIGHTLY

Readers often conclude that they want documents, such as reports, to be brief; a better intention is to make things succinct – that is, short but containing all the essentials to inform in an understandable way. Do not include irrelevancies nor aim for comprehensiveness, since it is rarely (ever?) an option. This means selection is important. You need first to decide what to write and what to omit. This is why planning is an important part of getting any document right.

Similarly, writing style also affects length; a convoluted style will fill more pages. The ability to write tightly is essential for longer documents

COACHING SESSION 36

Making it succinct

To practise writing tightly, look at the phrase below and see how many words you can eliminate without changing the sense.

'In spite of the fact that he was successful, it did not take him long before he was sorry that he had used so many words.'

It is worth taking a minute or two to try this, writing out a new and shorter version below and aiming to at least halve the word count, currently 26. This may involve rewriting rather than just shortening.

Here are two more sentences if you want to see if you can improve:

'One of the main consequences of rising property values is that it will be more difficult for people to afford new homes.' (22 words)

'John did not pay any attention to the results because he did not have very much confidence in the analytical techniques.' (21 words)

Note: Suggestions as to how each can be shortened appear separately below.

Making it succinct

Back to Coaching Session 36: The first sentence to be attempted was 26 words long. The following, encapsulating much the same message, consists of only 10.

'Although he succeeded, he soon regretted using so many words.'

I used this as an exercise on a training course not so long ago and one inventive participant reduced it still further – to 3 words: 'Successful, but verbose' (and it very nearly does capture the full message of the 26-word original version!). Certainly this is a good skill to develop.

The phrase above is not, of course, set out as the only 'right' way of approaching this; there are many options and as always circumstances will dictate what is best.

Reducing, again by more than half, the other two example sentences you might get:

1. 'Rising property values will make home-buying more difficult.' (8 words)
2. 'John ignored the results because he distrusted the analytical techniques.' (10 words)

You might look too at other things you have written recently and see if they contain sentences or paragraphs that are too long, that can in fact easily be abbreviated and made to read better while conveying the same meaning. Try picking one or two to rewrite.

COACH'S TIP

Find the right balance

There is an important balance to be struck here. If you omit salient parts, then meaning and intention may well be diluted – the message is left incomplete and lacks power. Make something too long, however, and people switch off, skip through and do not read it all. The answer? If in doubt, it is better to write more, rather than omit salient facts, which could reduce the likelihood of achieving your intention. But aim to write tightly.

REPORTS

Reports come in many forms: feasibility studies, research reports, staff appraisals and many more. Here we focus on the general principles. First, the greater the length and/or complexity, the more important it is to prepare carefully: to set clear objectives and focus appropriately on the reader. Greater length also demands a clear structure.

Structure: example 1

The simplest structure one can imagine is to have a beginning, a middle and an end. Indeed, this arrangement is what a report must consist of, but the argument or case it presents may be somewhat more complex.

To take a typical example, imagine a report of an examination of something (a process or new initiative, say) setting out its analysis and recommendations. Such may fall naturally into four parts:

1. Setting out the **situation**
2. Describing the **implications**
3. Reviewing the **possibilities**
4. Making a **recommendation**.

The two structures can coexist comfortably (in fact, each section may need its own beginning, middle and end); the overriding consideration is logic and organization.

Looking at an example helps spell out the logical way an argument needs to be presented if it is to be clearly communicated.

Imagine an organization with certain communication problems, a report making suggestions to correct this might follow the following broad sequence:

1. The **situation**: This might refer to both the quantity and importance of written communication around, and outside, the organization. Also to the fact that writing skills are poor, and no standards are in operation, nor has any training ever been done to develop skills or link them to recognized models that would be acceptable around the organization and help people be effective.
2. The **implications**: These might range from a loss of productivity (because documents took too long to create and had to constantly be referred back to clarify), to inefficiencies or worse resulting from misunderstood communications. It could also include dilution or damage to image because of poor documents circulating outside the organization, perhaps to customers.
3. The **possibilities**: Here, as with any argument, there might be many possible courses of action, all with their own mix of pros and cons. To continue the example, these might range from limiting report writing to a small core group of people, to reducing paperwork completely or setting up a training programme and subsequent monitoring system to ensure some improvement took place.

4. The **recommendation**: Here the 'best' option needs to be set out. Or, in some reports, a number of options must be reviewed from which other people can choose. Recommendations need to be specific: addressing exactly what should be done, by whom, and when, alongside such details as cost and logistics.

This is just one example. The next coaching session asks you to consider the precise structure that suits examples of the kind of document you write.

Before moving to that you can consider another structure, shown below.

Structure: example 2

A completely different example concerns explaining necessary action.

Instructions must be clear, especially if no verbal explanation is possible. So what might suit is:

1. **Define the task**: A description of what must be done, and why, to put it in context; this must be stated in familiar terms.
2. **A motivational note**: It may be important to reassure people that something is possible and to spell out what is to be achieved by the whole exercise – describing its importance.
3. **A chronological list**: A step-by-step list of what must be done, showing why something comes next, exactly what to do and flagging any warnings associated with the particular stage.

   Note: It may be useful to test this out, getting one person to follow the instructions and making sure they have no problems, before using the document on more people.
4. **Visualization**: This may be incorporated into stage 3: some tasks are made simpler by the use of diagrams or other visual representations to make things completely clear.
5. **Feedback**: A final section may look ahead, first suggesting what to do if there prove to be problems, prompting feedback or linking to other standing instructions.

This is clearly completely different to a report assessing a situation and making recommendations, but then the range of possibilities here is wide.

COACHING SESSION 37

Devising an appropriate structure

Decide upon an example of a typical report you have to write and think about the structure it could best follow (the smaller number of broad sections – as described above – into which it will fall).

1. The document's purpose:

2. The most suitable structure:

At all stages generalizations should be avoided. Reports should contain facts, evidence and sufficient 'chapter and verse' for those in receipt of them to see them as an appropriate basis for decision or action.

With the overall shape of the argument clearly in mind you can look in more detail at the shape of the report itself. The way in which it flows from the beginning to the end is intended to carry the argument, make it easy to follow and to read, and to make it interesting – even surprising and/or memorable – too, as necessary, along the way.

Two special features of reports are useful: **Appendices** and **Executive Summaries**. These can be defined thus:

Appendix:

An appendix removes material from the main text and places it at the end of a report; this allows the main content to be read without distraction, for instance without getting bogged down in detailed figures before the full case for something has been presented, and yet it also allows readers to check further details as and when they wish.

Executive Summary:

This is a summary in the conventional sense but is put at the beginning of a report (rather than at the end, as is a traditional summary) to provide an overview of what follows; essentially it says, 'here's why what follows is worth reading'.

Similarly, a long document must look right. It needs: adequate space and headings, clear numbering and clear emphasis (this latter delivered by graphic devices ranging from italics to boxed paragraphs).

PROPOSALS

This is a form of report that must also persuade. A proposal that is only inadequate in some small detail compared to one from a competitor may easily be placed second. Your proposal may be rated less impressive or appropriate by only a whisker – but you still lose out. So the quality of written proposals is vital.

Proposals may vary. Sometimes agreement comes after sending just a page or two of text by email. At other times a proposal may need substantial documentation as part of the process of gaining agreement. Such a process may be long, costly and multi-staged with proposals playing a sequential part along with meetings and more.

In other words, people can say no to a poor proposal and decide not to move on to complete the process. Because this is harsh, but true, whatever kind of proposal is necessary, it must be done correctly.

First, let us define terms.

Quotations versus proposals

What exactly is meant by the words 'proposal' and 'quotation'? Although they are sometimes used in a way that appears similar, in sales terms they mean something very different.

Proposals have to explain and justify what they suggest. They normally make recommendations, they certainly should assume that their job is to persuade.

On the other hand, a quotation is normally a much simpler document. It simply sets out a particular - usually requested - option. They say that something is available and what it costs. They assume, rightly or wrongly, that the sales job is done and that persuasion is not necessary. This may be true, especially in known situations. But many quotations should have more, sometimes much more, of the proposal about them.

Here we look at more complex proposals, though the principles concerned might also act to beef up any quotations you use and may be useful to other writing tasks too.

Choice of format

There are two main overall approaches to the format of proposals. Sometimes a letter, albeit maybe a longish one, is entirely appropriate. Indeed, sometimes doing more than this can overstate a case and put the recipient off. It is seen as over-engineering. Alternatively, what is necessary is much more like a report, though one with a persuasive bent.

A further form

This is the *discussion document*: a document for a stage before a proposal. Classically this sets the scene for a meeting, dealing with background and defining areas and ideas to be discussed at a meeting. Like all such documentation, exactly how it is written is vital to its success. A subsequent proposal, dependent on the discussion document being accepted, is thus an extension of this when both are involved.

Consider the main forms in turn, and when and why each may be appropriate.

Letter proposals

This starts with a first sheet set out like a letter, which begins, 'Dear... 'It may be several pages long, with a number of subheadings, but it is essentially less formal than a report-style proposal. This style is appropriate when:

- a more detailed proposal is not needed, because there would be insufficient content, or an over-formality
- the objective (or request) is only to summarize discussions that have taken place
- there are no outstanding issues (unsolved at prior meetings, for instance)
- there is no threat of competition.

Where these, or some of them, do not apply another approach is safer or necessary.

Formal proposal

This is a report-style document, usually printed and bound in some way and thus more elaborate and formal (colour and illustrations may also be involved). Such is appropriate when:

- recommendations are complex
- what is being sold (or asked for) is high in cost (or, just as important, will be seen as being so)
- there is more than one decision-maker, a committee, a recommender and decision-maker acting together or some other combination of people who need to confer and will thus see exactly the same thing
- you have not met some of those who will be instrumental in making the decision
- you know you have competition and are being compared.

Number of copies

Here's an important question. How many copies of a proposal should you send? The short answer is to ask and send however many are then requested.

In many businesses it is common for there to be multiple decision-makers or influences. Where this is even suspected it is doubly wise to ask how many copies of a proposal will be required. If you have seen, say, two people and the answer is three copies, maybe there is someone else you need to be aware of and more questions (or even another meeting) become the 'order of the day' before you move on. One way or another, you have to find out the role any additional people play and make sure that the proposal addresses them as well as others.

In anything to do with persuasion and selling, the reader and their views must naturally rank highly. What they want should rightly influence the kind of proposal you submit. Ask people questions such as:

- How formal should it be?
- What sort of detail is expected?
- How long should it be? (I have known cases where vastly longer documents than required have been submitted because this question was not asked.)
- How many people will see it? (See tip above.)
- By when do they want to receive it?

You do not have to follow their answers slavishly, but must make a considered judgement. For example, if you are dealing with someone you know, they may well suggest not being too formal. But, if you know you have competition and they are in discussion with other people, it may still pay to do something more formal than a letter.

In a comparison between a letter-style and more formal proposal, the former tends to look weaker, especially when related to value for money.

Timing

Timing is worth a particular mention. It is naturally good to meet people's deadlines, even if in some cases it means burning the midnight oil. However, it is likely that people want your proposal to reflect your considered opinion. Promising that on a complex matter in 24 hours may simply not be credible. Too much speed in such a case can cast doubts on quality and originality.

This is especially true of anything complex or creative, and when solutions are positioned as being truly bespoke. In consequence, it may occasionally be politic to delay something, asking for more time than you actually need to enhance the feeling of tailoring and consideration when it arrives. It's good to have time in hand for contingencies too.

So, at this stage you know something about what's needed, you know who is involved in the decision (i.e. those who will read whatever you write) and when the proposal is wanted.

COACH'S TIP

Be prepared

Remember the need for preparation: add in any time that composing such a document demands you spend with colleagues – in discussion, brainstorming, whatever – and set aside sufficient time to do a good writing job (and check you have done so). Once the document is sent, then – for good or ill – it must stand on its own feet.

Certainly once something has been sent, then you have to live with it. You cannot reasonably telephone a correction later or send a 'revised page 7' to be slotted in by the recipient. With all that in mind, let us now turn to see how the content should be arranged and dealt within a proposal.

Proposal content and arrangement

While the format and certainly the content of a proposal can vary, the main divisions are usually best described as:

1. The introduction (usually preceded by a contents page)
2. The statement of need
3. The recommendations (or solution)
4. Areas of detail (such as costs, timing, logistics, staffing and product or technical specification)
5. Closing statement (or summary)
6. Additional information (of prime or lesser importance, in the form of appendices).

Each section may need a number of subheadings and their length may vary depending on context, but they form a convenient way of reviewing the key issues about the construction of a proposal and are thus now commented on in turn:

Title/contents page

When there is any complexity, a proposal needs the equivalent of a book's title page. This states who, or which organization, it is for and what it is about. This page can also give the contact details of whoever it is from (which, if not here, certainly must be somewhere in the proposal) and, on a sales proposal, some people like to feature the logo of the recipient organization on it, as well as their own.

This should be followed by a sheet on which the contents of the proposal are listed and which gives the page numbers. It may make it look more interesting, and easier to navigate both as and after it is read, if there are subheadings as well as main headings, especially if the main headings have to be bland and generic.

Note: The headings that follow below are descriptive of the functions and role of the sections, not recommendations for headings you should necessarily use; these are often better when descriptive or memorable.

Introduction

Remember that a proposal is a persuasive document. The opening must command attention, establish interest and lead into the main text, making people want to read on. As the introduction has to undertake a number of important yet routine tasks, it may be best to start with a sentence (or more) that is interesting, rings bells with the reader and sets the tone for the document.

Thereafter there are a number of other roles for the introduction; for instance it may need to:

- establish the background
- refer to past meetings and discussions
- recap decisions made to date
- quote experience
- acknowledge terms of reference
- list the names of those involved in the discussions and/or preparation of the document.

As none of this is as interesting as what follows (if it is then you do have a problem!), this section should concentrate on essentials and be kept short. Its final words should act as a bridge to the next section.

Statement of need

This section needs to set out, with total clarity, the brief in terms of the need: why the proposal is being written. It describes the scope of the requirement, and may well act to recap and confirm what was agreed at a prior meeting about what the proposal would cover.

It is easy to ask why this section should be necessary. Surely someone who has asked for a proposal knows what they want? Indeed they have perhaps just spent a considerable amount of time telling you exactly that. But this statement is still important. Why?

Well, its role is to make clear that you do have complete understanding of the situation. It emphasizes the identity of views between the two parties and gives credibility to your later suggestions by making clear that they are based firmly on the real – and individual – needs that exist.

Without this it might be possible for someone to assume that you are suggesting what is best (or perhaps most profitable) for you; or simply making a standard suggestion.

This section is also of key importance if the proposal is to be seen by people who were not party to the original discussions; for them it may be the first clear statement of this picture. Again this part should link naturally into the next section.

Recommendation or solution

This is likely to be the longest section and needs to be logically arranged and divided (as do all the sections) to make it manageable. Clear and informative headings are needed. Here you state what approach you feel meets the requirements. This may be:

- standard, in the sense that it is a list of, for example, recommended approaches/products that you have discussed and sell as a standard solution; or
- 'bespoke', for example as with the approach a consultant might set out to instigate a process of change, implement training or indeed almost any of the many tasks consultants perform.

In either case this section needs to be set out in a way that is 'benefits-led', spelling out the advantages and making clear what the solution will mean to, or do for, the reader as well as specifying the details and/or technical features. Thus do not just list what you will do – describe what the result will be or how a stage will move things forward once completed.

Note that the total job here is threefold: to explain, to do so persuasively and also to differentiate. Never forget, when putting together a proposal, that you may well be in competition and what you present will be compared, often closely, with the offerings of others. A focus on the needs is usually the best way to ensure readers' attention; nothing must be said that does not have clear relevance.

COACH'S TIP

Internal considerations

Competition implies market competition, and it is easy to imagine a potential customer comparing a sales proposal with that from a competitor. But the same principle is involved within an organization too: for instance, you may write to someone asking for funding for some update, expansion or new development. The money you seek no doubt comes from a finite pot and thus your case will not simply be reviewed on its merits but it will be compared with other ways in which the money could be spent. It pays to bear this in mind as you write.

One further emphasis is particularly important here: individuality. It is so easy to store standard documents on disk these days, and indeed it may be possible to edit one proposal into a new version that does genuinely suit a similar need elsewhere (though double, double-check that you have changed everything necessary, for example, names and any other individual references; I received a proposal once that referred to me as Margaret half way through!). But, if a proposal is intended to look tailored it must do just that and there must be no hint of it seeming standardized.

This is sufficiently important to re-emphasize – bespoke proposals must never seem standard in any sense. Someone may well know that you write similar documents, but will still appreciate clear signs that you have prepared something 'tailored just for them'.

Only when this section has been covered thoroughly should you move on to refer to costs, because only once it is appreciated exactly what value and benefits are being provided can people consider costs in context.

Costs

All costs must be stated clearly, and not look disguised.

Spreading the cost description

One technique for presenting the figures is useful (disguising without disguising so to speak) and that is amortizing costs – describing something as £1,000 per month, rather than £12,000 for the year; or describing and costing stages separately – such as preparing and conducting training.

The necessary detail must be there, including any items that are:

- options
- extras
- associated expenses.

All must be shown and made clear. Something that is found to cost more than someone first thought tends to make you ill-regarded thereafter, and may preclude winning repeat business or gaining agreement next time.

Leaving aside pricing policy linked to sales proposals, do note that:

- price should be linked as closely as possible to benefits
- this section must establish or reinforce that you offer value for money, not just state figures baldly
- invoicing details and trading terms often need including, and must always be clear; mistakes here tend to be expensive (in the UK remember to make clear whether price is inclusive of VAT)
- overseas, attention must be given to currency considerations
- comparisons may need to be made with competition or with past projects
- range figures (necessary in some kinds of offering) must be used carefully (do not make the gap too wide and never subsequently go over the upper range figure).

Look carefully at how you arrange this section; it is not just facts and numbers, it must be as persuasive as any other part of the document. And note that costs used internally must be as well presented as price is externally to customers.

A question often asked is: 'Won't some people turn straight to the "costs" section?' Yes, without a doubt this happens – indeed, it is only realistic to assume that some (most?) clients will look at this page or pages before reading anything else.

Certainly for such people there needs to be sufficient explanation given, including cost justification and, above all, clear benefits, linked in here. Just the bald figures can be very off-putting.

This section must not only deal with its discrete topic, it must act to persuade the client who starts by reading the costs section that it is worth turning to the front and reading through from the beginning. Write it to achieve just that.

To reinforce points made here about costs, let me quote John De Forte and Guy L. Jones, who are co-authors of *Proposals, Pitches and Beauty Parades* (Pearson). They focus primarily on the most complex areas of proposing, those where competitive tendering is the best description of what occurs. Here the presentation of price (they focus on fee businesses) is perhaps even more important, but their advice is good for any situation:

'Treat it (presenting the price) as an opportunity to convey positive messages about your commitment to giving value for money and how you intend to help the client monitor and control costs; try to show that you want the service to be as cost-effective as possible... Apart from giving the fee itself, describe also the basis of charging and, if it is a long-term assignment, how fee levels might be determined in the future or when it would be appropriate to review them. If a detailed fee analysis is required, this may be better dealt with in an appendix.'

Additional details

It may be necessary to deal with certain additional topics separately here, as mentioned above: timing, logistics, staffing, etc. Sometimes these are best combined with costs within one section. Not if there are too many perhaps but, for example, costs and timing go well together, with perhaps one other separate, numbered, section dealing with any further topics before moving on.

The principles here are similar to those for handling costs. Matters such as timing must be made completely clear and all possibilities of misunderstanding or omission avoided.

COACH'S TIP

Bespoke

Bear the need for individuality and a tailored approach in mind; for instance, in services where people on a project are part of the package, a biographical note about yourself or colleagues needs to be tailored to any specific proposal.

Summary or closing statement

The final section must act to round off the document and it also has a number of specific jobs to do. Its first, and perhaps most important, task is of course to summarize. All the threads must be drawn together and key aspects emphasized.

A summary fulfils a number of purposes it:

- provides a useful conclusion for all readers and should ensure the proposal ends on a note that they can easily agree is an effective summary. Because this is often the most difficult part of the document to write, it is also a part that can potentially impress disproportionately. Readers know good summarizing is not easy and they respect the writer who achieves it. It is taken as a clear sign of professional competence;
- is useful too in influencing others around the decision-maker, who may study the summary but not go through the whole proposal in detail;
- ensures the final word, and the final impression left with the reader, is about benefits and value for money.

In addition, it can be useful to:

- recap key points (as well as key benefits)
- stress that the proposals are, in effect, the mutual conclusions of both parties (if this is so)
- link to action, action dates and details of contact (though this could equally be dealt with in a covering letter)
- invoke a sense of urgency (you will normally hope for things to be tied down promptly, but ultimately need to respect the prospect's timing).

There is also what is called an **Executive Summary**, just as with a report. This is a summary placed at the start of a document to do much the same job as one at the end. In part it is a matter of taste (or of what readers want – and you can ask), and sometimes you can utilize both.

The only other guide that seems useful is that a traditional summary (at the end) is best for a decision-maker. They will read it through and this positioning provides the most logical explanation. For recommenders or others less involved the executive summary may be preferred. Whichever is used it must be well written, and remember – a short final word remains necessary even when the main summary is placed early on.

Appendices

An important element can be appendices. It is important that proposals, like any document, flow. The argument they present must proceed logically and there must be no distractions from the developing picture. Periodically, there is sometimes a need to go into deeper detail. Especially if this is technical, tedious or if it involves numerous figures – however necessary the content may be – it may be better not to let such detail slow and interrupt the flow of the argument.

Such information can usefully be referred to at the appropriate point, but with a note that the 'chapter and verse' of it appears in an appendix. Be specific, saying, for example: 'This detail will be found in Appendix 2: Costs and timing, which appears on page 21'.

This arrangement can be used for a variety of elements: from terms and conditions of business to details inherent in a project (for example, a proposal about a computer systems project might list recommended hardware details at the end).

Covering letters

A proposal is a detailed document and it is sometimes questioned whether such needs a covering letter. The answer is clear – yes, it does – always. In part it is a courtesy, yet the content of the letter is important, and more so for more complex situations and more elaborate proposals. It will, if it is interesting, be the first thing that is read. It sets the scene for the rest of the message. So it must say more than 'here is the promised proposal' (a compliments slip could do that) and is a useful place to add emphasis, perhaps instilling a sense of urgency, touching on results or setting the scene for any meeting you hope will follow.

Next, assuming proposals arrive safely and are read, there is another possibility: that their use may link to, which needs some thought at the writing stage.

The presentation of proposals

Some proposals are posted just like a letter; once in front of the prospect they must do their work alone, though they may be followed up in numerous ways: by letter, email, telephone and so on (persistence here can pay dividends).

COACH'S TIP

To email or not to email

Consider carefully the emailing of proposals. This can be satisfactorily done, especially in sending something to people you know well (or if requested), but it does not put something as smart as a bound document on their desk. Speed may be of the essence sometimes, but you can always follow up an email with a copy sent physically and this may be well advised.

Sometimes you know that complex proposals, especially those involving more than one person in the decision, will be the subject of formal presentations. These can happen in two main ways:

- The proposal is sent, then a presentation is made later to those who have (or should have!) read the document

- The presentation is made first, with the detailed proposal being left as a permanent reminder of the presentation's content.

If such an arrangement is made in advance, then the proposal needs to reflect what is to happen.

For example, you may need more detail in a proposal that has to stand on its own than one that will follow a presentation. It might sometimes be possible (with agreement) to delay completing the proposal until after a presentation; thus allowing the inclusion of any final elements stemming from any feedback arising during the presentation meeting. Alternatively, you can issue a revised version at this stage, either amending a draft or adding an appendix.

Certainly there should be a close parallel between the two entities so that it is clear how anything being said at a presentation relates to the proposal. Rarely should any of the proposal be read out verbatim.

COACH'S TIP

PowerPoint

The use of PowerPoint slides is a standard presentation device these days, but a major fault in presenting is the reading of lengthy text from the screen (usually done while looking at the screen and away from the audience). If you use extracts from a report or proposal, cutting and pasting the text into slides, you compound the likely problem. Resolve not to do this; slides should be originated separately and above all be brief.

What is usually most important is for additional explanation, examples and exemplification of what has been written to be given verbally.

It may cause confusion if, say, a proposal with eight main headings is discussed at a meeting with nine or ten items being run through (certainly without explanation). It is helpful if you can organize so that the job of preparing the proposal and the presentation overlap and are kept close.

COACH'S TIP

An extra copy

A final idea here may be useful: more than one company I know print out – for themselves – a 'presentation copy' of the proposal in a larger than normal format or type size. This enables it to be easily referred to by someone standing in presentation style at a meeting. It also gives additional space to annotate the document with any additional notes that will help to guide the presentation along precisely. One caveat here: just remember that page numbers will be different on the different versions and do not let this cause confusion.

ONLINE RESOURCE

Presenting the proposal

Many documents need to be persuasive; proposals certainly do. They do not act on their own – they link closely to a presentation (what may in sales terms be called a 'pitch'). Proposals, like a pitch, should address likely objections.

www.TYCoachbooks.com/BusinessWriting

Two rules

These are obvious but nevertheless still likely sometimes to be overlooked.

- Make sure every proposal looks good. Use plenty of headings, bold type where appropriate and make it look professional. Do not cramp it – if it is being passed round the client organization, adequate space for annotation is useful.
- Check it carefully – very, very carefully. It is worth reiterating the earlier example of the consulting firm that had a photocopy of the title page of a proposal returned to them. It was sent in an envelope without even a compliments slip. The name of the client's organization was incorrectly spelt; it was ringed in red and underneath was written, 'No thank you!'

COACHING SESSION 38

Proposal writing

Think of and note a topic that suits.

Proposal topic:

____

____

____

____

____

____

____

Then take the topic above and make a few notes about the content that would be necessary in each section.

1. The introduction (usually preceded by a contents page)

2. The statement of need

3. The recommendations (or solution)

4. Areas of detail (such as costs, timing, logistics, staffing and technical specification)

5. Closing statement (or summary)

6. Additional information (of prime or lesser importance, in the form of appendices)

BROCHURES AND LEAFLETS

Now we spare a few words about other specialist documents, which may be used in a number of ways: for example, brochures distributed by salespeople, leaflets you display in a reception area or items for staff information or used from the sales office or for direct mail. There is, however, no reason why such material should be suitable for everything and you may need to produce dedicated material, tailored specifically to one specific task.

Here we focus primarily on (corporate) brochures sent by post whether en masse or one at a time (though the principles are similar for copy written for a website or newsletter).

In either case, the brochure is unlikely always to set out to tell people 'everything there is to know' about the organization, product or whatever. Rather it may prompt a desire for discussion. Too much information can even have the effect of reducing responses.

One hotel, sending direct mail to promote its conference business, found that the numbers of potential clients coming to inspect the hotel doubled when they replaced a short letter and glossy comprehensive brochure with a longer letter, no brochure and an invitation to visit (it seems the people seeing the full brochure felt no need to visit, it seemed that they felt they could see what the place was like).

Content selection

The most important thing is to match your intention – what you want readers to do – with the amount and nature of the information you decide to include. This should be a conscious decision and what is to be omitted is as important as what is included.

The production of brochures generally is an area of increasing professionalism and great care is needed in defining the objective, creating the right message and making sure the brochure looks good and reflects the image that the organization intends to project. The days of the bland, general brochure, one very similar to those of other industry competitors, which describes the chronological history of the firm and everything it does and is intended to be used for everything, are rapidly passing.

What is needed now is the ability to match each objective in every particular area with something specifically designed for the job. This may mean producing separate brochures for each product in a range. It may mean that any 'corporate' brochure is a folder with separate inserts aimed at different target groups or different types of customer. It may mean a revised brochure every year if it is always to be correct and current. It may even mean a difference between the sort of brochure that is right to give a prospective customer after a preliminary meeting and the sort that is suitable to present to an intermediary who may have a role in, say, recommending you to others. It is 'horses for courses', and the specific individual uses and objectives should precede and dictate the writing and the content.

Content first

I notice that when I have undertaken copywriting of brochures for clients that the format of the brochure often seems to dictate the copy. It is best to think about the message you want to put over first and then see how it can be accommodated and in what, rather than say you see it as a brochure of a certain size and format and then try to squeeze the message into that. Note: Also avoid slavishly repeating a past format, again without consideration of the message.

For mailing purposes the brochure or leaflet concerned must be specific to the objective set for the particular promotion. Brochures may need to be reasonably self-standing; after all they may get separated from any covering letter (though the two together almost always produce a better response). However, the wording of the total content – letter plus brochure – needs to hang together, to produce a complete and integrated message; this is true of design and message.

Overall, what must be created is something that is accurately directed at a specific group, with a clear objective in mind. This may seem basic; of course, promotional material is there to inform, but it must do so persuasively. That is the primary purpose. But this does not, as comments on persuasiveness made clear, mean moving to something that is inappropriately strident (which might in any case be self-defeating), and it does mean putting a clear emphasis on customer need and benefits (what things do for people, rather than simply what they are).

Essentially, a customer-focused approach, well designed for its purpose, is the rule.

COACHING SESSION 39

Avoid introspection

A simple exercise that will reveal any over-introspection is to take an existing document about your organization (or its products or services) – a corporate brochure makes a good example – and read it through. As you do so, keep a count of all the times a paragraph, sentence or thought starts introspectively, that is with the words 'we', 'I', 'the firm' (or similar), and so on. Compare this with the number of times the word 'you', 'the customer/client', or similar is used. Space is allowed below simply for the count.

There should of course be more of the latter (and if there are many more introspective words or phrases then the problem is pronounced). You may conclude that some change (or even a total rewrite) is necessary.

Overall, promotional documents must:

- look good (though good design is much more readily available than good writing)
- be practical (for example for mailing and filing if you hope people will keep it)
- be illustrated in some way (this almost always enhances appearance)
- be readable, interesting and relevant with the message being put across in a punchy, perhaps novel, way.

There are a few rules to be observed about brochures and those rules are sometimes made to be broken. This is because they must be creatively constructed to reflect the image of the organization graphically, differentiate it from its competitors and aim the chosen message directly at the identified target group.

But the copy continues to be more important than anything.

Many brochures have clearly had a good deal of money spent on their design and print, but the text is dull or inappropriate. Start with the copy – taking on board all the principles set out here – and then design the brochure as a vehicle to carry your message.

MAKING DOCUMENTS LOOK GOOD

Despite the importance of words, remember that the end product should be neatly – and, of course, clearly – presented. This principle applies to every kind of document, but perhaps especially to longer ones.

Basics first: any message must look right. It must be attractively laid out, grammatically correct and well presented. This is especially important if the message is in any way difficult (controversial, needing to persuade, etc.) since it then gives the impression that it has originated from a professional source.

To start at the simplest end of the spectrum with letters; the letterhead itself is important to the image: an up-to-date yet not 'over the top' design should be aimed for, and this is not easy. Subjective judgements are involved. Ultimately, it is a matter of opinion and in smaller organizations this can sometimes mean a safe compromise that may dilute impact.

Consider, too, whether your standard letterhead is right for every purpose (for instance, direct mail purposes may demand something different). For example, one with all the contact information at the foot of the page allowing a heading and perhaps more to go at the top.

COACH'S TIP

Email

Emails are, of course, different from a letter on a formal letterhead, but the way they look and the information their standard features contain is also important. This may need some checking out and thought (especially if this has not been reviewed for a while). While some emails are routine and can be as simple as you like, others are not.

Additional finishing touches that can add impact include the following:

- Position text on the page according to the length of it. It is unattractive if there is a huge expanse of white below a very short letter. Position it lower down, in that case, or consider having two sizes of letterhead paper printed and put short letters on the smaller sheets. Or use a larger font perhaps
- Create 'block' (rather than indented) paragraphs, with double spacing between each paragraph for greater clarity and smartness
- Leave at least 4 cm at the foot of the page before going onto a second page; leave a bigger space to avoid having only one or two lines (plus farewells such as 'yours sincerely') on the second page. A good deal of business material ends up annotated in some way, so more space actually makes this easier for people to do
- Allow enough space on a letter for the signature, name and job title. It is better to carry the letter over onto another page, than cram it in at the bottom
- At the foot of the last page, note all the enclosures mentioned in the text and sent with the letter
- Staple the pages together to avoid losses
- Always number pages (useful to make this a rule for every document)
- Number the paragraphs when a lot of points have to be covered
- Underline all headings or (better) make them bold.

In addition: layout must reflect the style, the reader and the emphasis of the points being made. For example, it can bolster a persuasive message by helping create emphasis and put over a feeling of efficiency.

Graphic emphasis can help keep people reading, guide them through longer texts and simply create a feeling of accessibility that promotes readability. Such emphasis can be made in a number of ways, with:

CAPITALS

<u>Underlining</u>

    Indenting

Bold type

While these features should not be overdone, they can be useful and, in whatever form and combination you select, should be well placed. White space is as important as text, and the overall effect is designed to make the text seem accessible both as you flick through on first picking up the book and on reading it. It is very different to the 'textbook' style of old. The overall layout, especially the number of headings, is important to its appearing accessible and readable.

Anything that looks a mess is likely to be taken as a mess, ill thought out and giving its reader little confidence in what is to come. The reverse is true, too: a well presented document will always enhance its content, particularly early on when potential readers are still deciding how much attention to give it and how seriously to take it.

NEXT STEPS

Everything that has gone before applies to the special cases reviewed in this chapter and longer documents such as reports clearly present their own challenge and need careful consideration in both their writing and presentation. One additional factor that applies especially, but not exclusively, to longer documents is the way you deal not only with words but also with numbers. This is worth a short chapter, as follows.

TAKEAWAY

This section is designed to give you a moment to take stock. You may decide to read on, return to earlier coaching sessions or make some notes of progress to date and factors likely to be important to you in the future. Some notes in response to the questions here may prove useful as you proceed.

Writing tightly is a most useful skill, are you content you can do this adequately or is it something to practise further?

The structure of longer documents is always important; is it worthwhile spending more time writing this particular kind of document?

Are you sure you are not writing in a way that seems to project a feeling of standardization, when the recipient will respond best to something they see as tailored for them?

A final, but important, element of any document is a professional look. Assess whether you might improve in this area.

9 DEALING WITH NUMBERS

OUTCOMES FROM THIS CHAPTER

- This short chapter concludes by assessing the effectiveness of many business documents that feature numbers: that is statistics, performance figures, finances and more. First it describes the ways in which numbers are perceived, then sets out ideas that will allow you to bolster an argument or case by using numbers in a clear, powerful way.

THE NATURE OF NUMBERS

Number 'blindness'

Figures and statistics often form an important element of many a document. They can explain, clarify – or confuse. The job is normally to make sure they do not confuse, of course, but perhaps it should be acknowledged that sometimes numbers are thrown around precisely in order to confuse. For example, someone in a meeting might rattle through a mass of disparate costings in the hope that the crux of how expensive a plan is will not be dwelt upon. Similarly, the complexity of figures may be used on a grander scale: in marketing people talk about 'confusion pricing' – a pricing structure of such complexity that it makes it difficult for a customer to undertake comparisons with competitors (mobile phone tariffs are an example of this with which many people are familiar).

In this chapter, however, the concentration is on the positive: using numbers effectively in the course of business but especially in writing. Taking a positive view is important because many people:

- assume numbers will confuse them; they lack – or believe they lack – skills in numeracy (finding anything from percentages to break-even analysis difficult) and, because they switch off when figures appear, they need to be motivated to appreciate them
- have a blinkered attitude to figures. For instance, they can take in numbers and concepts on the scale of their own bank balance, but corporate figures confuse by their sheer size
- are overwhelmed by the sheer volume of figures.

Such attitudes demand that particular approaches are necessary.

MAKING NUMBERS CLEAR

Figures always need to be presented in a well-considered way if they are to enhance a message. The first principles are to:

- select what information is presented, identifying and focusing on key information and leaving out anything that is unnecessary. This can mean for instance that information needs to be tailored; the detailed chart included in a report may be inappropriate to use for other purposes and must be abbreviated. Many slides used as visual aids are overcomplicated when simply taken from a page in a document
- separate information, for example, into an appendix to a report, so that the main message includes only key figures, and the overall flow of the case being made is maintained while more details can be accessed if required
- separate too information and the calculations that arrive at it. This can be done using appendices or by such devices as boxed paragraphs in a report
- select the appropriate accuracy as you present figures. A high level of accuracy sometimes helps understanding, or is simply important, while on other occasions it can confuse and ball-park figures better suit
- repeat to help get any message across. With numbers natural repetition - for instance, going through them verbally and issuing something in writing as well - can make all the difference
- proofread. Numbers must be checked perhaps even more carefully than words in written material; remember that one figure (and one decimal point) wrongly typed might change things radically.

Making it work

A single example should illustrate the variety of ways to describe things. Consider sales results: the state of play might be described in five different ways (and you may be able to think of more):

1. 'Sales are up.' No detail may be necessary
2. 'Sales are up about 10 per cent.' A broad estimate may be fine
3. 'Sales are up 10.25 per cent.' The precise figure may be important
4. 'Sales are up about £10,000.' The financial numbers may be more important than the percentage (and can be presented with the same different emphasis as just described for percentages). In addition, what the figures refer to must be made clear. For example: 'Sales of product X are up 10.25 per cent for the period January - June 2015.' Language can, of course, change all such statements - 'Sales are up substantially' - maybe, as here, just by adding one word
5. Present information in a way that makes it easy for people to understand it; for example in graphic form.

COACH'S TIP

One little word

One little word is surprisingly often misused. Note that it is nonsense to say, as is often heard: 'Sales are up about 10.25 per cent' – the word 'about' only goes with round figures and estimates or forecasts; the more decimal places are involved the worse the grammatical error.

COACHING SESSION 40

Varying the description

The last point shows that the precise way in which something numerical is described is important and that the way chosen should reflect exactly how you want it to come across. Select something other than the sales figures factor example above, preferably something numerical you actually must work with, and list five (at least) differing ways in which the base facts might need to be described.

Number factor selected:

____

____

1. ____

2. ____

3.

4.

5.

GRAPHS AND CHARTS

The old saying that a picture is worth a thousand words has real meaning here and this principle relates directly to numbers of all sorts. A graph can convey an overall picture, one immediately understood – sometimes literally at a glance.

Often, two graphs work better than a more complex single example, and of course they must be set out to maximize the visibility of the information they display. Thus they need to:

- be an appropriate size
- use different colours when possible and when this helps; carefully chosen colours too, picked to contrast one against the other
- be suitably annotated, with thought being given to what text appears on the graph itself and what is separate (in a key at the foot of the page, perhaps)
- work effectively, or be adapted so to do, if they are to be used separately as visual aids, when legibility is doubly important.

Consider the various kinds of chart and graph that can be used, these include:

Bar charts

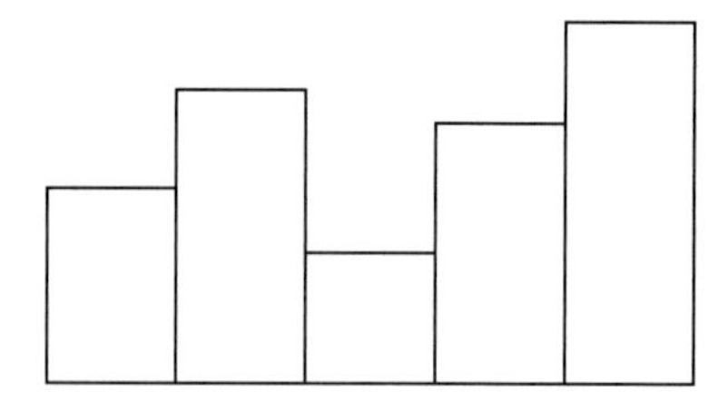

The example makes the effect of this clear; scale can again be varied for emphasis and colour or shading can help too.

Tables

	1	2	3	4	5
A					
B					
C					

This term encompasses anything that sets out figures in columns; they can be of varying degrees of complexity.

Pie charts

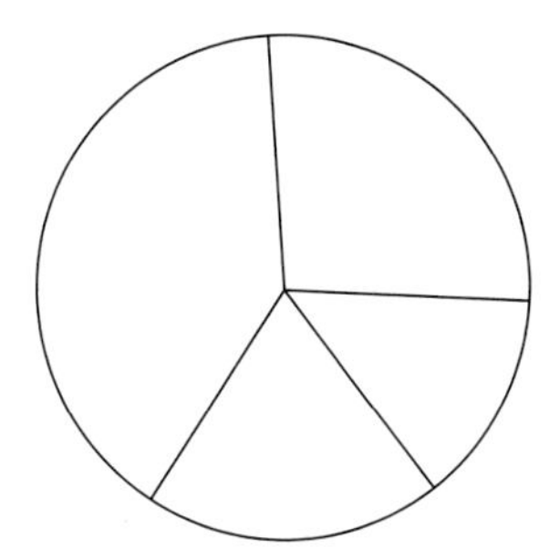

This is an especially visual device and can make many things much clearer than, say, a table and certainly a description in words/numbers alone.

Graphs

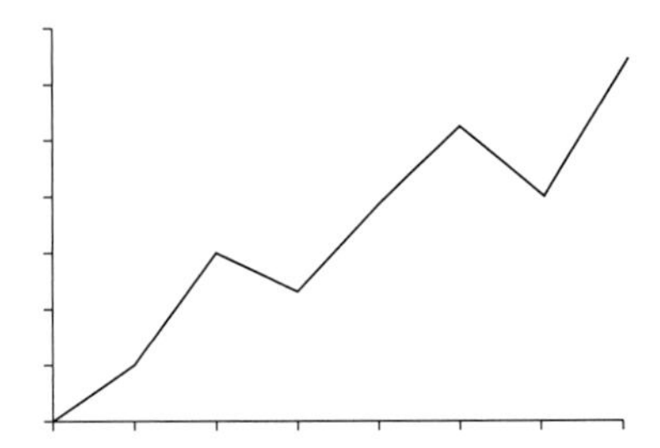

These are useful to show the differences of quantities varying over time. Care must be taken to select scales that give the picture you want (there can be a lot of trickery with this sort of graph – something to bear in mind when you are interpreting them rather than deploying them).

Project timetables

A	Phase 1	2	3	4	
B	1	2	3		
C	1	2	3	4	5

← Time →

A device to help people visualize the timescale of projects with multiple and overlapping stages.

Flowcharts

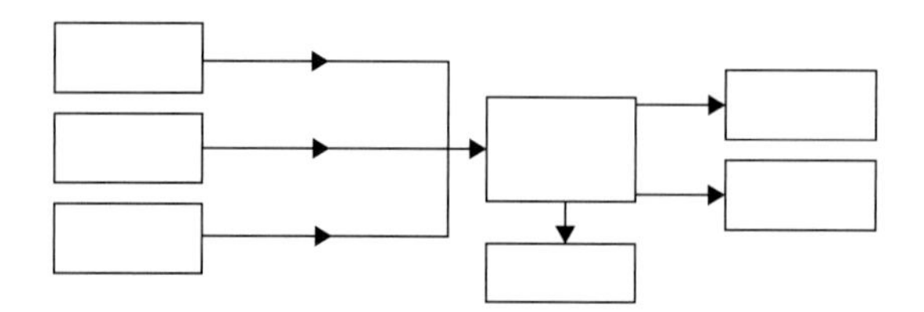

These can be more elaborate and allow the presentation of a more complex picture – useful where interrelationships are concerned.

Keep it simple

All these graphic devices benefit from being kept as simple as possible. Complexity, which includes trying to demonstrate too many different things (such as overall sales, sales by product, profitability and so on…) on one graph, can quickly drown out clarity. There is a danger here if charts are taken from elsewhere and incorporated into something like a report, they may need adapting and simplifying or split into two).

Sometimes a compromise is necessary between the 'perfection' of a lovingly created graph and the time (and thus sometimes cost) of producing it. Despite this, the greatest danger is using few, or poorly, executed devices when the information they present makes their use necessary. It is true to say that pictorial representation of some sort added to, say, a report can swing an argument or further agreement.

The power of such devices can be considerable.

As an example of minimal information in graphic form let's return to the pie chart. If you consider the impact a written document has and consider the contribution of the words it uses and the sub-text that is conveyed in addition by its tone and style as people read between the lines, you can visualize a pie chart:

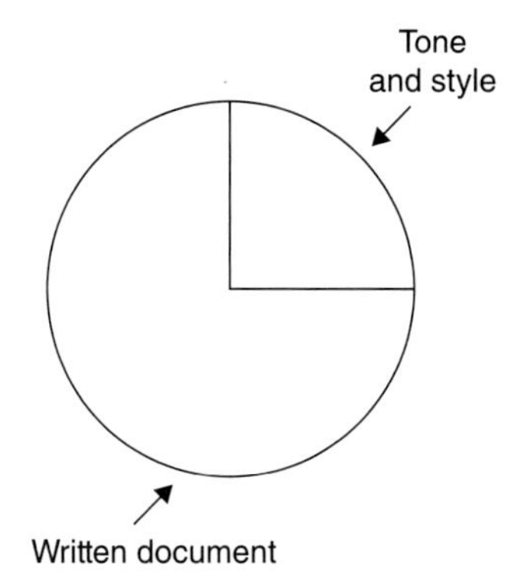

The point made here is that the sub-text is significant (the chart is not displaying an exact figure, of course); seeing this, it may be easier to take the lesson here on board and resolve to think of this aspect of the impression you give as you write your next document, than it is just by reading a sentence here making the point in words only.

COACHING SESSION 41

A graphic example

Take an example of a numbers-orientated point you must make and consider the best way to augment it graphically. Note the words to include and how they work with the graphic device.

LANGUAGE OF NUMBERS

Certain factors are important here:

- **Pace**: in verbal communication you may need to slow down a bit when dealing with numbers and build in more, and longer pauses. In writing the same effect can be achieved by scene setting and not going straight to the bald numbers
- **Signposting**: this can focus attention – 'let's look at this carefully, it can be confusing and the details are important'
- **Checks**: you can test your approach in conversation, reading out loud what you have written and seeing if people keep up – or look at you blankly
- **Precision**: exactly the right accompanying word can make a difference, ensuring that figures are taken exactly as intended.

  For example: 'note that this figure is an *estimate*' or 'This is the position *today*'
- **Nonsense**: some statements using numbers can in effect be nonsense. For instance, you often hear advertisements on the television saying things like – 'now more than 70 per cent'. High percentages of something good may automatically sound good, but pose the question – compared with what? It might be a competitor, or an earlier version of the product; or it might just be unclear.

Another technique that can help is that of making comparisons. This can be done in various ways. For example, many numbers, not least financial ones, involve comparisons with other periods of time – 'this is more than last year' and 'administration costs are down, though customer service ratings are up'.

Similarly, comparisons can be made simply to aid description. This is especially helpful if figures are very large or otherwise beyond the day-to-day experience of those for whom the numbers are being laid out.

One aspect of this is simply in the words, you may select a comparison that is accurate and an important detail of what is being described. Thus an office extension might be described as –'the size of a tennis court' – when even an accurate number of square metres (and this may be there too) might fail to create an easy-to-grasp and accurate picture.

COACH'S TIP

Exaggerate

Sometimes it helps to exaggerate – describing a serious shortfall in revenue, say, as 'akin to the national debts of most of South America'. The exaggeration is extreme and everyone recognizes that this is done only to highlight the importance, and size, of the actual figure being discussed (which should also be included).

This links to what is called 'amortizing', which means to spread a figure expressing it as smaller units, which are divisions of the whole. For example, an annual cost of, say, £1,680 can be described as '£140 per month', 'only £140 per month' or 'not even £150 per month'.

Language is always important, of course, but perhaps its role when linked to numbers is especially so (and, because of a distaste or uncertainty about numbers is inclined to be overlooked or glossed over). It is worth a short digression to describe an example that illustrates just what a difference can be made with care.

A travel agent is essentially a service and people business. In one particular firm, with a chain of some 30 retail outlets across several counties, competition meant the business was failing to match its targets. Good market conditions meant it was something that a more active, sales-oriented approach could potentially cure.

Initially, management's approach to this was to draw attention to the problem at every level. (Wordy) memos were circulated to all staff. The figures: the sales revenue planned for the business, the amount coming from holidays, flights, etc. were substantial figures; even the shortfall was some hundreds of thousands of pounds.

The result? Well, certainly the sales graph did not rise. But, equally certainly, morale dropped. People went from feeling they worked for a successful organization to thinking it was – at worst – floundering and feeling that the fault was being laid at their door. The figures meant little to the kind of young people who manned the counters – they were just unimaginably large numbers to which they were wholly unable to relate personally.

With a sales conference approaching, a different strategy was called for. The large shortfall was presented as a series of smaller figures – one per branch. These 'catch-up' figures were linked to what needed to be sold, in addition to normal business, in order to catch up and hit targets. It amounted to just two additional holidays (Mum, Dad and 2.2 children) per branch, per week. This was something staff could easily relate to – and which they felt they could actually achieve. Individual targets, ongoing communication to report progress and some prizes for branches hitting and beating these targets in a number of ways were all documented to complete the picture.

The result this time? The numbers slowly climbed. The gap closed. Motivation increased with success in sight. And a difficult year ended with the company hitting the original planned targets – and motivation returned, continuing to run high as a real feeling of achievement was felt.

The key here was communication. The numbers and the difficulty of hitting the targets did not change. The perception of the problem, however, was made manageable, personal and – above all – was made to seem achievable. The results then showed that success was possible. All that was necessary was to present the figures in a different way – one that reflected the realities of the situation and that was directed at staff on their terms.

A final thought linked to language. Consider two further factors:

- In verbal communication the tone of voice helps get a message over clearly. Do you, for instance, want a '10 per cent increase' to sound good or bad? Additional words may be necessary to achieve the right emphasis in writing.
- Numbers, and the words that accompany them, can be presented with different visual emphasis too. In bold type, or italics perhaps, or in a larger type face.

COACHING SESSION 42

Creating the right emphasis

Take an example of a document and make a list of the various emphases you might want to make. For example, with a change in performance figures you might want to stress the importance, prompt action, promote care or highlight that something was good, bad or excellent.

Nature of the numbers (e.g. sales figures)	Possible emphases

NEXT STEPS

Numbers can either enhance communication or they can confuse and, at worst, result in the whole communication falling on stony ground. The key to success is to:

- recognize the role and importance of numbers within the message
- recognize the difficulty some people have with numbers
- choose a style of communication that highlights them appropriately, both literally (e.g. bold type) or by appropriate emphasis
- illustrate figures wherever possible, for instance with graphs
- be especially clear in what is written, to use powerful description and sufficient detail for matters to be understood.

You are very nearly at the end, and the next step is to pull everything together and summarize so that you can go on your way better able to write in a way that achieves what you want.

TAKEAWAY

This section is designed to give you a moment to take stock. You may decide to read on, return to earlier coaching sessions or make some notes of progress to date and factors likely to be important to you in the future. Some notes in response to the questions here may prove useful as you proceed.

Do you find numbers difficult, and if so in what specific ways?

Can you identify ways in which you use figures and practise putting over information appropriately?

Do you provide information in a visual form to make it easier for those you write for to understand, and if not can you change this?

Similarly, are you using language to give precisely the right emphasis to your descriptions?

10 QUICK HELP

Now some final words by way of summary, but first I promised the answer to the problem of the odd paragraph in Coaching Session 2. The text is repeated here:

'As you scan this short paragraph, try to spot what is unusual about it. Half an hour is normal for many to find a solution that is both logical and satisfactory to its originator. I do not say that anything is "wrong" about it, simply that it is unusual. You may want to study its grammatical construction to find a solution, but that is not a basis of its abnormality, nor is its lack of any information, logical points or conclusion. If you work in communications you may find that an aid to solving this particular conundrum. It is not about anagrams, synonyms, antonyms or acrostics, but it is unusual. So, why is that?'

The answer to why the paragraph is odd is simply that, unusually, the paragraph contains no letter 'e'. This is the most commonly used letter in the English language; normally, writing any amount of text without one would be quite difficult. This was intended only as a bit of fun, but, if you want a moral, it shows that attention to language can teach us something.

KEY THINGS TO BEAR IN MIND

It was Samuel Johnson who said: 'What is written without effort is in general read without pleasure.' You might not want to give people pleasure (literally) from your business writing, but you assuredly want to put over your messages successfully and in a way that achieves objectives.

So what to do? Business writing in all its forms is not something most people who work in organizations can avoid. It goes with the territory, as they say. One option is to muddle through, regarding it as a chore, getting by, but perhaps missing the opportunities the process presents. In some ways this option seems almost attractive. Some people convince themselves that the effort of doing otherwise is not worthwhile or is too time consuming. Some remain convinced they cannot change what they regard as a 'fixed' style.

Given that it must be done, it follows that the best approach is to learn to do it well – and thereby achieving the greatest likelihood of getting what you want. I have certainly intended the text to show clearly that you can do this. It may involve a little study, some care and practice but, be assured, you can turn out excellently written documents.

It is regularly the case that documents have too much relying on them to be treated anything other than seriously. If results are not to suffer and if your profile, and prospects, as the writer are to be as you wish, it is something that demands attention.

Doing it well does not just happen, of course, and getting to grips with skilled writing is easy to understate or underestimate (I have seen it said that writing is easy; all you need to do is think of all the words you know and put some of them down in the right order). It certainly requires some effort, especially if you are set in your ways. But all the factors that make for success are essentially common sense.

SIX KEY FACTORS

To tie down what needs to be done to a short list of key factors (while accepting that there is detail within each area), I would highlight the following:

1. **Objectives**: You need to know why you are writing and what you want to achieve by so doing; writing without a clear objective gives you an impossible task and makes it highly unlikely that readers will applaud your efforts
2. **Preparation**: With a clear purpose you can proceed to this next stage (including any background research that is necessary); this is key, but can be straightforward. It is well described by the old phrase about engaging the brain before the mouth – or in this case usually the typing fingers!
3. **A systematic approach to writing**: When you get down to writing you need to assemble the words by employing a logical, systematic approach (such was suggested in Chapter 3). Find and refine your own version of this and it will stand you in good stead – not least, by teasing apart what to write from how to put it
4. **Structure**: All business documents need a clear, logical structure – not just a beginning, a middle and an end, but whatever the particular nature of an individual document demands. A sound, logical structure creates a core that

carries the content, begins to make it clear and attractive to readers who see it as a sign of a professional job and a likely easy read

5. **Language**: words, phrases, grammar, punctuation and more – overall every aspect of the use of language matters. Being grammatically correct. Language matters to the clarity of the message and it matters in terms of what the tone and style you adopt say not only about the message but also about your organization and about you. You need to work at both aspects. If you have clear objectives and say what you mean, succinctly, and build in appropriate description and style, people are more likely to want to read what you have written. **Note:** The boxed section that follows, a light-heartedly put classic reminder to correct and proper writing, may amuse, remind you of things to remember or to explore in further detail.

Some memorably put writing rules:

- Don't abbrev things inappropriately
- Check to see if you any words out
- Be careful to use adjectives and adverbs correct
- About sentences fragments
- Don't use no double negatives
- Just between you and I, case is important
- Join clauses good, like a conjunction should
- Don't use commas, that aren't necessary
- Its important to use apostrophe's right
- It's better not to unnecessarily split infinitives
- Only Proper Nouns should be capitalized. also a sentence should begin with a capital and end with a full stop
- Use hyphens in compound-words, not just in any two-word phrase.
- In letters reports and things like that we use commas to keep a string of items apart
- Watch out for irregular verbs that have creeped into your language
- Verbs has to agree with their subjects
- A preposition isn't a good thing to end a sentence with
- Avoid clichés like the plague

6. **Check**: check, check and cheque (sic) again. And try to do so having left what you have written for a moment, and without the kind of deadline that you should never have accepted and that makes inadvertent carelessness almost inevitable.

   There is often just too much hanging on the success of what you write to skimp on this and, as most of us have found, it can be as important for a one line email as it can for a multi-page report.

WHAT NEXT?

Bearing these key principles in mind, any necessary new habits can quickly build and replace the old. You will find that with some consideration and practice you will write more easily, more certainly, and in a way that is well matched to your purpose and to your intended readers. This, in turn, will make it more likely that you will achieve your objectives. Even the best writing will not rescue a poor case, but it will strengthen whatever case you put over, making it more likely to be studied, considered and acted on in the way you intend.

As a final element here right at the end of the book you may want to spend a few minutes on the Action Plan that follows; this gives you an opportunity to link the messages of this book with your work and upcoming tasks to ensure that you make the most of the experience.

You will also find that with practice your writing takes less time. Good preparation particularly can remove the need for elaborate rewriting and editing on material that should have been closer to its final form in the first place, if only it had been given more thought. If writing can be achieved promptly, it becomes less of a chore and this may itself act to allow you to think about it in a more constructive way.

There is, after all, a certain pleasure in locating just the right phrase to make a point; more in finding it has worked and been well received.

Professional writers suffer as much as anyone in trying to articulate in a way that makes them happy; I know I do! But they also report it to be a satisfying process, even if this is with hindsight: one writer, Michael Kanin, is quoted as saying: 'I don't like to write, but I love to have written.'

So the next document you have to write presents a particular opportunity. Having read this book, you will know something of the factors that help create good business writing. Whatever your current style and standard, there may be new things you can try, old things you can aim to change and improve upon.

I will give the last word to an especially prolific author, Isaac Asimov (who wrote nearly 500 books, mainly science and science fiction). Asked what he would do if told he only had six months to live, he answered simply in just two words: 'Type faster.'

Clearly he was someone who enjoyed writing. But his reply is also a good example of the power of language. Think how much his brief response says about the man and his attitude to life, his work and his readers.

I will not end by wishing you good luck with your future writing; I have, in an a way, spent 50,000 words explaining that good writing is not a matter of luck – but I wish you well with it.

ACTION PLAN

It has been made clear during this text that business writing is a skill that demands some care and consideration. It also benefits from practice. Having been through the book you may have things – changes in your practice – in mind now that you can implement easily, but there may be other things that you feel it is worth exploring further, working on or which need to become a habit. It is most likely to make a difference if you work at such things in a manageable way, taking a little time (you are no doubt busy), so as a final act perhaps I may suggest that you make a list here of any points you want to revisit or practise so that you can return to them in future to complete the process.

FURTHER READING

Bill Bryson, *Troublesome Words* (Penguin) 1984

John De Forte and Guy L. Jones, *Proposals, Pitches and Beauty Parades* (Financial Times) 1993

Martin Manser, *Good Word Guide* (Bloomsbury) 1988

Nick Oulton, *Killer Presentations* (How to Books) 2003

Lynne Truss, *Eats, Shoots & Leaves* (Profile) 2003

Keith Waterhouse, *English our English* (Viking) 1991

INDEX